Iron Chef

Iron Chef

THE OFFICIAL BOOK

Compiled by Fuji Television, Inc.

Edited by the Staff of *Iron Chef*

Translated by Kaoru Hoketsu

BERKLEY BOOKS / NEW YORK

B

A Berkley Book
Published by The Berkley Publishing Group
A division of Penguin Putnam Inc.
375 Hudson Street
New York, New York 10014

PRINTING HISTORY

Fusosha Japanese hardcover edition / 2000
Berkley hardcover edition / May 2001

The Penguin Putnam Inc. World Wide Web site address is
www.penguinputnam.com

LIBRARY OF CONGRESS CATALOGING-IN-PUBLICATION DATA

Ryori no tetsujin taizen. English.
    Iron chef : the official book / by Fuji Television ; translated by Kaoru Hoketsu.
        p. cm.
    ISBN 0-425-18088-3
        1. Cookery, International. 2. Cookery—Competitions. I. Hoketsu, Kaoru. II.
Fuji Terebijon, Kabushiki Kaisha.
    TX725.A1+
    791.45'72—dc21
                                                                                00-065120

PRINTED IN THE UNITED STATES OF AMERICA
10   9   8   7   6   5   4   3   2   1

Contents

IRON CHEF

All chefs are equal in the eyes of an ingredient

Foreword

OCTOBER 10, 1993, PROVED TO be an unforgettable evening not only for myself, the host of the Gourmet Academy, or for all the members of the Academy, but for the entire world.

It all started when a chef of Chinese cuisine, Go Maruyama, having won the preliminary rounds, challenged our Gourmet Academy's First French Iron Chef, Yutaka Ishinabe. Since then, many glorious battles have been fought in our beloved Kitchen Stadium. Battles were fought and gourmet dishes created, the memories of which are now forever etched in our minds.

Some 893 foie gras, 54 sea breams, 827 Ise shrimp, 964 matsutake mushrooms, 4,593 eggs, 1,489 truffles, 4,651 grams of caviar, and 84 pieces of shark's fin were eaten, to mention just a few statistics. These delicacies were used in abundance, bringing the total grocery bill to more than 843,354,407 yen (about $8,000,000). The damage does not stop there. After having consumed a total of 2,389,995 calories, I myself was forced to undertake a strict regiment of physical exercises.

Now, just as the ancient Chinese Han warrior Ssu Ma Chien wrote the *Shiki,* I have decided to record the history of 6 years in Kitchen Stadium. I shall dedicate this book, along with my profound gratitude, to my seven Iron Chefs, to all the chefs who stood up to challenge them, and to every member of my staff.

I hope that every person who shall read this book will share with me my philosophy that "cuisine is the greatest form of art to touch upon a human's instinct."

—TAKESHI KAGA,
Chairman of Gourmet Academy

Introduction
to the American Edition

IF YOU KNOW ENOUGH ABOUT *Iron Chef* to pick up this book, you know this is not going to be your ordinary behind-the-scenes look at a popular television show. It's going to be stranger, more exciting, and just plain better. This book is about accomplished professionals at the height of their fields who turned the culinary world upside down with their talent. It is filled with the exclusive stories and recipes behind mouth-watering meals never before attempted, meals filled with lobster, foie gras, truffles, and other delicacies. But it is also the story of grown men in ridiculous costumes wrestling live octopuses while announcers breathlessly fill us in on the action. And therein lies the genius. *Iron Chef* is not only the most ambitious gourmet cooking show in the history of television, it's also the most outrageous.

Inside these pages, you'll hear from the man who dressed the chefs

in their trademark costumes. You'll get insight from the first person to say, "Hey, wouldn't it be interesting if, let's say, a cabbage was placed on an elevator-like platform and brought up on stage?" You'll learn the challenge of building the world's greatest cooking arena for each and every show. You'll receive the exclusive recipes to Chairman Kaga's favorite dishes, peruse Hattori's Prestige Menus, and hear directly from the Iron Chefs—all seven of them—for the first time.

And no matter what you think you know, you're going to learn something new.

Can you name all the American and Canadian challengers (there have been six)? Did you know that Announcer Yukio Hattori twice battled Iron Chefs in Kitchen Stadium? That Kaga once boycotted a match in anger because his Iron Chefs kept losing? That there have been numerous "tag team" matches involving four Iron Chefs at one time? That the wife of second Iron Chef Japanese Koumei Nakamura was so embarrassed after he lost a battle that she wouldn't leave the house? If you've just watched the show on The Food Network, you probably don't even know that second Iron Chef Japanese Koumei Nakamura exists . . . yet.

As Chairman Kaga said, this is the complete history of *Iron Chef*. The book was created in Japan as the definitive *Iron Chef* book soon after the final program aired there in September 1999. It is a summation of everything that happened in the 6 years the show was on the air and a chance for everyone involved in the show to say their piece. For this edition, we've added material about The Food Network version of the show and the event that made *Iron Chef* a huge success in America: The New York Battle. But we've also left in a lot of material about a few people you've probably never heard of, but who are nonetheless important figures in the *Iron Chef* world. In other words, this is the *Iron Chef* book. No matter how many episodes you watch on The Food Network, no matter how many years you follow the show, it will never go out of date.

People have asked, Why not tailor a book just to the American version? To us, that's like asking, Why not substitute American actors for Hiroyuki Sakai and Chen Kenichi? Besides, it wouldn't be the whole story if we left out all this juicy material, right? In this book, we've done exactly what The Food Network has done. We've translated the original, then stood back and let the stars speak for themselves. There is no better way to get to know them, both as professionals and as human beings. At times this is touching, at times informative, at times even bizarre. But as Takeshi Kaga has said, "It's great to be known, but it's even better to be known as strange."

Enjoy!

Iron Chef

THE NEW YORK BATTLE

Can you smell

what Morimoto is

cooking?

THE NEW YORK BATTLE: FOR better of worse, it was the event that brought *Iron Chef* to the attention of America. Sure, many people had been watching the show for years, and Chairman Kaga and his merry band of chefs had traveled the world before—Hong Kong, Thailand, France, even New York for an informal tour—but this time it was different. This time the Iron Chefs were coming to New York City to do battle in a makeshift Kitchen Stadium in front of hundreds of screaming fans. And this time it was going to be broadcast into millions of homes in America via a 2-hour special.

What did Americans know about *Iron Chef* in June 2000? Well, they had most likely seen the commercials during Emeril Lagasse's popular cooking spectaculars. Most, though, had never bothered to watch the show, despite the fact many had heard *Iron Chef* was becoming a hit.

Others had heard of the fish head ice cream, the pig stomach casseroles, and the wanton butchering of live fish. Even more had been flipping channels at some point and come across the image of a grown man wrestling a rather large live octopus that is shown at the beginning of every show. And while many had stopped to watch and been hooked, many others hadn't bothered.

Until now.

The challenger, anointed by those in the know to defend the honor and prestige of American cuisine, was Bobby Flay, top New York chef and star of The Food Network's very own hit show *Hot Off the Grill*. Flay was an acknowledged master of American Southwestern cuisine, a style the Iron Chefs had never encountered before. Would this be a problem for the culinary men of iron? After all, the last American to enter Kitchen Stadium, Ron Seigel, had whipped Iron Chef French Hiroyuki Sakai in Battle Lobster. The tension mounted through an hour of hype, as Chairman Kaga was feted around New York, Kobe and Sakai thrilled the chefs-to-be at the Culinary Institute of America, and Japanese Iron Chefs Michiba and Morimoto were horrified into silence by the contents of a suburban woman's freezer.

The New York Battle itself had actually been filmed 2 months earlier, when on a cold March weekend New York City's Webster Hall, best known as a rock concert venue, was turned into the city's most fantastic cooking arena. With help from The Food Network and experts from Fuji Television in Japan, all the workings of a world-class kitchen— make that two world-class kitchens—were assembled, from the sinks and refrigerators to the multiple stoves to the more than 500 dishes, bowls, and cooking implements. The result was astounding, if not quite up to the level of the one true Kitchen Stadium. The background wasn't lavish, the Iron Chefs didn't ascend from the floor in a flourish and, even worse, midway through the battle challenger Bobby Flay was electrocuted by a combination of faulty wiring and a puddle of water.

Who would take it?

Whose cuisine would

reign supreme?

But nothing could dampen the enthusiasm of the crowd. As Kaga entered the arena and took his familiar place at center stage (as befits a medieval lord), they waved signs, whistled, chanted, and cheered. Challenger Bobby Flay, the great hope of New York, challenged Iron Chef Japanese Masahura Morimoto, the New York–based chef fighting for the other team. The crowd yelled appreciatively. Kaga theatrically summoned the theme ingredient, which descended slowly from the ceiling in the top half of a disco ball. The crowd went wild. The Chairman, with the formality of a baron and the style of a showman, smiled and boomed forth his famous catch phrase, *"Allez cuisine!"* . . . and Battle Rock Crab was under way.

The Great Cutting Board Controversy

The day after the show aired Stateside, the newspapers and water coolers of America were abuzz. While most of America was agog at what they had witnessed the night before, many die-hard fans (some of whom were reporters) were a little underwhelmed. The expectations had been, perhaps, a bit high. No lives were saved, no economies ruined, no rocket sent to Mars. And while it's true that without the interjections of famed sideline commentator Shinichiro Ota—"Fukui-san!"—the edge was off the

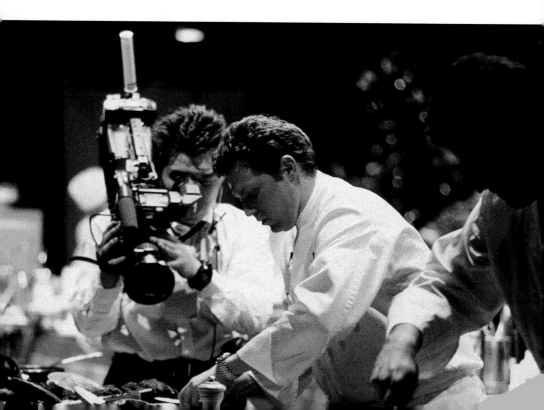

action, the knives had been dicing and the ingredients flying all the way to the final seconds. And that's the moment it had happened. When Bobby Flay, in classic American fashion, stood up on his counter to exhort the crowd and celebrate his culinary accomplishment, the true nature (and appeal) of the *Iron Chef* hit every American home.

Iron Chef Morimoto, with obvious agitation and without mincing words, dismissed Flay as a pretender. "In my country," Morimoto told America, "the cutting board is sacred. This man is not a chef." Not a chef? A sacred cutting board? Was he serious? Was this what the *Iron Chef*, this over-the-top spectacle, was all about?

The answer, of course, is yes . . . and no. The *Iron Chef*, as you will discover later in this book, is a deathly serious contest with reputations and careers on the line. The victor will gain the people's acclaim forever, but the loser will suffer the people's derision and mocking for . . . well, at least a few days. When Morimoto won this Battle Rock Crab, it was obvious to even the most casual viewer that it was a great relief. Having mocked Bobby Flay's professionalism, he couldn't turn around and lose to him in the world's most watched cooking competition. His reputation, his very livelihood, was on the line. And that's how it should be.

In Japan.

But this battle took place in America, and in America we want to see spectacle and pomp and wild action. We want to hear rousing music and watch vegetables ascend in a cloud of dry ice. We want to see a grown man in a sequined robe chomp into a yellow pepper again and again and again. We want to see (if not eat) octopus and eel and other bizarre animals. We want to cheer for a chef who will jump up on his countertop and wave a towel around his head. And that's what Bobby Flay gave us.

So in the end, we all won. Morimoto won because he proved himself a world-class chef. Bobby Flay won because he proved he's a fun guy to be around. America won because we got to watch a wonderful hour of

television, an hour that is repeated in more or less the same form several times a week. The Food Network won because the viewership of *Iron Chef* has tripled in the past year. We won because due to your enthusiasm we got the opportunity to bring this wonderful book to America. This book, in turn, makes the world an even more interesting place for fans of *Iron Chef.*

The Rest of the Story

While all that was going on, there was another aspect of the New York Battle that was equally interesting, but probably overlooked by most

Americans. As any fan of *Iron Chef* knows, Iron Chef Chinese Chen Kenichi, the lovable teddy bear of Szechwan cuisine, did not make the trip to America. Filling in as Kaga's fourth iron man of culinary skill was Rokusaburo Michiba. Michiba, dressed in his luminous blue robe, was the Japanese Iron Chef when the show first began airing in Japan. Although he retired midway through the program, he is a legendary and beloved figure in Japan. The New York Battle, however, was his first appearance on American television.

The presence of Michiba hinted at the long and intricate history of *Iron Chef*, a history that only now is coming to light in America. We have seen hints of it, for instance, in the attempts by the ultra-conservative Ota faction to take down the "Neo-Japanese" Iron Chef Morimoto. As the show progresses on American television, more and more characters like Iron Chef Michiba will enter the lives of American fans, and the story of Chairman Takeshi Kaga and his Iron Chefs will get deeper and more rewarding.

While several special battles are still planned, the majority of *Iron Chef* lore and legend has already been created. This book will take you back to the battles you have already seen. It will introduce you again to the men and women you have come to know and love. But it will do more than that. It will also tell you the rest of the story.

THE GOURMET ACADEMY

LIKE THE ACADEMY THAT PLATO founded in Athens, the Gourmet Academy was founded on a personal philosophy. In this case, it is my philosophy that "Cuisine is the greatest form of art to touch upon a human's instinct." As such, I have invested all of the worldly fortune I have inherited from my ancestors into the construction of Kitchen Stadium.

If memory serves me right, the great chef Béchamel served in the court of France's Louis XIV. He created the famous Béchamel sauce at Louis's banquet and was said to have greatly impressed the king. At around the same time, there was a chef in China by the name of Enbai. Enbai created the basis of Chinese cuisine within the grounds of Zuien, where it is said that over 300 ingredients, with the exception of tofu and pork, could be found. In Japan, we had the great Rosanjin Kitaoji. I dream of meeting these legendary chefs one day. In order to realize this

dream, even if just a little bit, I came up with the following rules of battle for my Gourmet Academy. Kitchen Stadium is a place to discover the great chefs of today, and a place for them to better themselves by challenging one another.

The Rules of the Game

The basic belief of the Gourmet Academy is that "Love is not what makes a great dish; it is the technique and artistry involved." Every week, a chef will challenge one of the three (later four) Gourmet Academy Iron Chefs to a culinary battle. Should a chef beat the Iron Chef in the preliminary battle, he or she shall be permitted a second battle, and should he or she win this battle as well, he or she will be awarded the honorary title of Iron Chef.

The theme ingredient will not be made known to either the challenger or to the Iron Chef until the time of the battle. The chefs must come up with a menu of at least three courses that utilizes the theme ingredient to its full potential. They have 1 hour only to accomplish this task. Three to four members of the Gourmet Academy will taste the meal and judge it. To be fair, I, as the host, shall not offer any opinions. Should the marks turn out to be equal, there will be a 30-minute rematch, after which the next meal will be tasted and judged.

Iron Chef Profiles

Awaiting the arrival of challengers in the world's only culinary battlefield, Kitchen Stadium, are the Gourmet Academy's Iron Chefs. These chefs are legendary figures, creating unforgettable dishes with only their knives and their vast knowledge to guide them.

The First Iron Chef of Japanese Cuisine: Rokusaburo Michiba

Using his belief that "There are no national borders for ingredients," Michiba utilizes numerous ingredients from all over the world to create his own special dishes. His belief has earned him the label of "rebel within the culinary world." Never losing his cool on the battlefield, he never shirks from any ingredient or from any challenger. He commands the respect of chefs from all walks of cuisine.

The First Iron Chef of French Cuisine: Yutaka Ishinabe

Ishinabe has been revered as the "God of sauces" within Japanese culinary circles. French cuisine in Japan is said to have advanced a good 10 years with his arrival. Always tasting the ingredients raw first, he then decides on the menu. Believing in only his tongue, his cooking is said to border on the artistic. He is referred to as being the "Visconti of the culinary world."

Iron Chef of Chinese Cuisine: Chen Kenichi

Kenichi's father, the late Chen Kenmin, was the first to introduce Szechwan cooking to Japan and is also responsible for having created the famous dish Shrimp in Chili Sauce. Since childhood, Kenichi has made his father's sacred kitchen his playground, and his every move, from the tossing of his wok to the adding of his spices, is said to be just like his father. His dishes, reflecting his belief that "Cooking is love," makes everyone feel joyous.

The Second Iron Chef of French Cuisine: Hiroyuki Sakai

Sakai is the chef responsible for having synthesized the Japanese kaiseki with French cuisine. His dishes reflecting the Japanese seasons and the esprit of France, are colorful; and he is often referred to as the "Delacroix of the culinary world." His genius is obvious in the way he creates extraordinary dishes at the spur of the moment. When not cooking, Sakai's hobbies include gymnastics (he is very good at the horizontal bar), deep-sea diving, and driving different cars.

The Second Iron Chef of Japanese Cuisine: Koumei Nakamura

Having been recognized by the first Japanese Iron Chef, Rokusaburo Michiba, he was crowned the second Japanese Iron Chef. He guards the tradition of the prestigious Japanese restaurant Nadaman, which was established in 1830. While respecting tradition, he is in no way bound to it and creates imaginative dishes that liken him to the ancient Chinese warrior Kung-Ming. True to his motto that "Without adventure, there will be no progress for a chef," he mixes tradition with the avant-garde, creating dishes that match no other in their depth.

Iron Chef of Italian Cuisine: Katsuhiko Kobe

The Enoteca Pinchiorri in Florence, Italy, is the epitome of Italian cuisine. Our fourth Iron Chef is a man who, by the tender age of 27, had mastered all the arts of Italian cuisine in the kitchen of this restaurant. He has rightly earned his nickname "Prince of Pasta." His youth and ardor have opened the door to a new era of Italian cuisine in Japan.

The Third Iron Chef of Japanese Cuisine: Masahura Morimoto

Morimoto leads the way to a new age of Japanese cuisine, as he has worked in New York, a true melting pot of cultures. His dishes, which incorporate all the essence of Chinese, Western, and Japanese cooking, represent a new age in "world cuisine." This revolutionary chef stands by his motto that "Cooking is entertainment" and does not forget to add spice and playfulness to his dishes. Morimoto enjoys golf, good clothes, and exercise, which matches well with his reputation as the "hunky" Iron Chef.

Iron Chef Timeline

Since its inception in 1993, numerous dramas have been born on this show. Here is the chronological history of the show that forever changed the culinary world.

Iron Chef History
1993

October 10

■ *Iron Chef* begins with the unveiling of Kitchen Stadium and the three Iron Chefs Michiba, Ishinabe, and Chen.

■ The program consists of two battles: the preliminary and the final battles. The time allocated for the final battle is 1 hour and 30 minutes.

October 17

■ The time allocated for the final battle is shortened from 1 hour and 30 minutes to 1 hour.

November 21

■ Preliminary battles are discontinued.

■ The Iron Chefs lose their first battle. Chinese chef Kazuhiko Tei becomes the first victor.

December 5

■ The battle of the Shu family: The number one apprentice of Shu and Shu's younger brother both lose against the Iron Chefs. Big brother Tomitoku Shu rises to avenge their losses and after two tries, finally wins against Iron Chef Michiba.

December 12

■ The first battle of desserts. The theme is Christmas.

December 19

■ Start of the special programs: The Christmas Special Battle.

1994

February

- **The blitz of the Kandagawa army: Toshiro Kandagawa, master chef of the Kansai region, sends his first challenger on February 16.**

- **After two of his apprentices lose, Kandagawa himself takes on the Iron Chef and wins against Kenichi in Battle Turbot.**

February 27

- **The debut of the new French Iron Chef, Hiroyuki Sakai. The first Iron Chef, Yutaka Ishinabe, is now an honorary Iron Chef.**

March 20

- **The first woman challenger appears at Kitchen Stadium.**

April 29

- The challenge of Yukio Hattori, the commentator: **Hattori, who covets the title of Iron Chef, challenges the chefs to a battle, but loses. Ambition undeterred, he awaits his next opportunity.**

July 22

- A summer holiday special, the Tag Match: **The French cuisine team, Joel Bruant and Furutaka versus the Japanese-Chinese cuisine team, Michiba and Kenichi. The French team is victorious.**

October 14

- **The first challenger from overseas, the number one chef from Hong Kong appears at the studio.**

December

■ The *Iron Chef* is nominated for the American Emmy Awards.

December 16

■ The second Christmas Dessert Battle.

December 23–January 2, 1995

■ The 1994 Mr. Iron Chef Contest: **A preliminary battle is fought among the Japanese, Chinese, French, and Italian successful challengers of 1993 and 1994; the winner battles against the number one Iron Chef, Michiba. Japanese cuisine chef Kandagawa is the winner of the preliminary battle. He battles Michiba, but loses. Michiba is crowned the 1994 Mr. Iron Chef.**

1995

January 27

■ **Valentine's Day Dessert Battle.**

March 31

■ The battle of the Iron Chefs in Hong Kong: **The first battle fought overseas, in the culinary capital of Hong Kong.**

■ **The battle is fought between Michiba, Chen, and China's best chef.**

■ **Hong Kong movie star Jackie Chan is present as a judge.**

May

■ The challenge from Club Mistral: **The Club Mistral, a group of young French chefs from France, challenge Sakai and Ishinabe.**

June 23

- Michiba, due to ill health, temporarily leaves the show.

August 11

- Michiba's return. Fights Battle Umeboshi.

August 18

- The second Tag Match: Italy's Salvatore brothers against the Sakai–Michiba team. The theme ingredient is tomato. The Iron Chef team wins.

September 8

- Noda Mínoru of Los Angeles's Hanabishi becomes the first American challenger to enter Kitchen Stadium. He proudly carries an American flag into his Battle Matsutake Mushroom against Michiba.

October 6

- **Iron Chef World Cup 1995 in the Ariake Coliseum: Four of the world's premier chefs in Chinese, French, Italian, and Japanese cuisine battle each other for the crown as the world's best chef. The Japanese representative, Michiba, wins the crown.**

October 13

- **Change of rules: four judges preside now and, in case of a tie, a 30-minute rematch is to be fought.**

November 17

- **Number of challengers reaches 100.**

- **Kandagawa is chosen as the most memorable challenger.**

December

- **The *Iron Chef* is again nominated for the American Emmy Awards.**

December 22–January 3, 1996

- The 1995 Mr. Iron Chef contest: **Audiences are invited to observe this battle. The price of tickets doubles, making it a true premium ticket. A fierce battle is fought between Michiba, Sakai, and Kenichi; and Michiba is   the 1995 Mr. Iron Chef.**

1996

January 3

- **Rokusaburo Michiba announces his retirement.**

February 9

- **Valentine's Day Battle.**

March 1

- **The new Japanese Iron Chef, Koumei Nakamura, makes his debut.**

April 12

- **The Ultimate Iron Chef Battle in France: Using a French château as the stage for this battle, Iron Chefs Nakamura and Sakai challenge the great chefs of France.**

- **The Iron Chefs are beaten.**

October 11

- **The Ultimate Iron Chef Battle in Peking: The Forbidden City is the stage for this battle between the four Chinese cuisines from**

Szechwan, Canton, Hong Kong, and Peking. Chen Kenichi, the Szechwan chef, defeats the three other chefs.

November 15

■ **Wayne Nish of March in New York City becomes the second American challenger. He fights Battle Apple against Sakai.**

December 13

■ **Christmas Dessert Battle.**

December 31

■ **The Ultimate Iron Chef Battle: The first Japanese Iron Chef and second Japanese Iron Chef, Michiba and Nakamura, battle against each other on New Year's Eve, 100 guests acting as judges.**

■ **The theme is osechi, the traditional Japanese New Year's dish. The entire episode is broadcast live.**

■ **Nakamura wins this battle.**

1997

March

• **Return Match 1–4. A rematch is held between four defeated challengers of French, Japanese, Italian, and Chinese cuisine and the Iron Chefs.**

June 13

• **Italian Iron Chef Katsuhiko Kobe is introduced.**

August 8

• **Summer Holiday Special Tag Match between the Iron Chefs: The first Tag Match fought between the Iron Chefs. The battle is**

fought between the European cuisine team, Sakai and Kobe, and the Asian cuisine team of Nakamura and Chen. Watermelon is the main ingredient. The winner is the European team.

August 22

- **Dessert Battle. The reigning champion of desserts, Sakai, is finally defeated.**

August 29

- **The first match fought without being judged. Reiten Kojima battles Nakamura.**

October 10

- **Iron Chef World Cup 1997 in Arashiyama, Kyoto: Using Arashiyama as the stage, four chefs, including Peter Clark from**

the United States, engage in a furious battle. Japanese chef Nakamura and the French representative, Alan Passard, fight one another in the final battle. The chefs tie.

December 12

- The number of challengers reaches 200.

December 19

- Christmas Dessert Battle.

1998

February 6

- Aritayaki Challenge: A hundred million yen's worth (about $905,000) of Aritayaki porcelain dishes were used in this battle.

February 20

■ Nakamura's retirement battle: **Yukio Hattori battles the Iron Chef for the first time in 3 years.**

February 27

■ **The third Iron Chef Japanese, Masaharu Morimoto, is introduced.**

April 10

■ Wedgwood Challenge: **More than fifty different types of Wedgwood plates worth 80,000,000 yen (almost $750,000) are brought into the studio.**

August 28

■ The 2000th plate Special Battle: **A special match, in celebration of the 2000 dishes that the host had tasted, is fought. The themes for this battle are the host's favorites: pork, terrapin, and banana. A dream team led by Sakai and Chen cook up a glorious feast.**

September

■ **Ota Tenchi no kai is started, marking the beginning of Morimoto's agony.**

■ **That group of chefs guard the traditional form of Japanese cooking.**

■ **The team challenges Morimoto to four battles, of which Morimoto loses three, but finally wins the last battle.**

October 9

- Ron Siegel of Charles Nob Hill Restaurant in San Francisco defeats Sakai in Battle Lobster, becoming the only victorious American chef.

December 25

- Christmas Battle.

1999

February 12

- Valentine's Day Battle. The world's premier patissier, Hinnobu Tsuguchi, arrives on the scene.

March 5

- Michiba travels to New York. Morimoto, working in New York, has faced a slump after a year as the Iron Chef. Kaga dispatches Michiba to help him.

March 12

- A match between the second Japanese Iron Chef Nakamura and Morimoto is fought in order to teach Morimoto the ways of the Iron Chef.

May 21

- Kaga, angered by the decline of victories of the Iron Chef, boycotts this match.

- Hattori steps in as the host, and Iron Chef Chen Kenichi manages to win. Successive victories for the Iron Chefs follow after this.

May 28

- Iron Chef in Indonesia. At the request of Jakarta's King Jog, Michiba and Morimoto travel to Indonesia and cook up a magnificent banquet.

July

- The Food Network begins broadcasting *Iron Chef* in the United States.

July 2

- Michael Noble from Vancouver's Metropolitan Hotel becomes the first and only Canadian challenger. He challenges Morimoto in Battle Potato.

July 30

- The number of challengers reach 300.

- A challenger from La Tour D'Argent battles Iron Chef Chen Kenichi. After a rematch, the battle ends in a tie.

September 10–24

- The Battle for the Strongest of all Iron Chefs. The Iron Chefs battle each other.

- Chen and Sakai end up at the final battle, and Sakai wins the coveted title.

■ **The Battle for the World's Best Chef: France's number one chef, Alan Passard, and Sakai fight the battle for this title. Sakai wins.**

■ **This is the last regularly scheduled battle to occur in Kitchen Stadium.**

2000

January I

• **The Millennium Match. The first Special Battle since the closing of Kitchen Stadium.**

March 12

• **The New York Battle airs in Japan. American Southwestern cuisine chef Bobby Flay challenges Morimoto. The battle takes place in New York City's Webster Hall. Morimoto wins.**

June 25

• **The New York Battle airs in the United States. The Food Network promotes it as a 2-hour special. The rest, as they say, is television history.**

The Specialty of the Gourmet Academy: The Host's Choice of the 10 Best Dishes

If my memory serves me right, the number of dishes born over the 6 years of the *Iron Chef* is 2,500. Based on my wish to "taste with my own tongue the dishes hailed as art," I have invested all of my worldly fortune into the building of this culinary battlefield. I feel honored to have been able to taste the countless artistic dishes, prepared by the divine chefs of today.

Undoubtedly, many of the dishes introduced in Kitchen Stadium are the epitome of culinary excellence. I believe that the numerous recipes I have acquired are invaluable assets to the culinary world. Thus I have decided, with the closure of Kitchen Stadium, to catalog these recipes for future reference.

I will introduce to you now the 10 most memorable dishes that I have encountered.* These recipes will surely become an invaluable fortune for the next generation. I hereby bequeath these recipes to all the people of the world.

*See the Gourmet Academy's Glossary of Culinary Terms on page 217 for definitions of unfamiliar terms.

Foie Gras Kanpon

Rokusaburo Michiba

The first Japanese Iron Chef, Michiba, cooked up this dish during his debut battle. Michiba likened the foie gras to ankimo that is used in Japanese cooking. He realized his own maxim that "Ingredients know no national borders." Foie gras mainly consists of fat. Elsewhere, fat is a delicacy, but in Japan and America, there is an averse reaction to anything fatty. In order to combat this negative image, Michiba prepared the foie gras with ponzu sauce to give it a fresh, light taste. With this dish, he has created a perfect harmony between the East and West, and has demonstrated to the world what the *Iron Chef* is all about.

200 g turbot

1 Chinese cabbage stem

Asatsuki (green spring onions), to taste

100 g foie gras

Flour, for dredging

VINAIGRETTE SAUCE

200 cc ponzu sauce

30 cc mirin

20 cc balsamic vinegar

50 cc daikon radish, grated

Moiji oroshi, to taste

Grated ginger, to taste

Slice the turbot into fillets for sashimi. Cut the stalk of the Chinese cabbage into bite-size pieces, and chop the asatsuki into 1¼-inch pieces.

Dredge the foie gras with flour, saute in a saute pan, and dice the foie gras.

Mix the ingredients for the vinaigrette.

Arrange the sauteed foie gras, Chinese cabbage, and turbot on a dish. Sprinkle asatsuki on top and pour the vinaigrette over it.

Thinly Sliced Sea Bream with Smoked Organs

Toshio Tanabe

This dish was created during the 14th contest Battle Sea Bream. The French cuisine chef Tanabe, a genius of fishes, created this dish. Though he lost against Michiba, I was deeply impressed by the taste of this dish. I have secretly named this dish "The Anatomical Chart of Sea Breams."

The objects placed around the sea breams are all organs. Tanabe has brought life into these organs, which are usually discarded. These organs, stewed in milk and then smoked, have been completely rid of any unpleasant odors. They are succulent, tasting like rich meat.

Tanabe, ever the genius, has taught me how to appreciate every bit of an ingredient.

1 sea bream

Milk, as needed

1 handful of cherry blossom tree smoke chips

Salt, to taste

Asatsuki (green spring onions), to taste

VINAIGRETTE SAUCE

10 cc red wine vinegar

100 cc salad oil

Shallots, to taste

Salt and pepper, to taste

Remove the liver, stomach, and intestine from the sea bream. Using a petty knife, squeeze out the insides of the stomach and intestines. In order to rid the organ of any odor, wash lightly with milk, and remove excess moisture with a cloth.

Place the cherry blossom tree smoke chips into a pot or saute pan, and place over fire. When the chips start to smoke, place the organs on a piece of aluminum foil and spread over the chips. Cover the pot. Once the organs are cooked (5 to 10 minutes), remove from the pot and set aside for cooling.

Fillet the sea bream, and slice into thin slices. Place the sea bream pieces on a plate (7 to 8 pieces per person), season with salt, and sprinkle asatsuki over it. Cut the organs into bite-size pieces. Arrange them around the sea bream.

Mix the ingredients for the vinaigrette sauce, and pour over the entire dish.

Roti of Homard with Vanilla Lindenbaum Flavoring

Pierre Ganiére

This dish was created during the battle fought at the Château de Balzac in France by the genius French chef Pierre Ganiére.

With the boom of culinary experimentation, many new types of herbs are being used today. However, I was surprised that lindenbaum could be used in a dish. I was not the only one to be surprised. The great French chef Joel Robuchon, who was present at the time as one of the judges, was also surprised by the use of lindenbaum, and he soon incorporated this herb into his dishes.

2 homards

Salt and pepper, to taste

Oil, for sprinkling

1 whole vanilla bean

Several leaves of lindenbaum

GARNISH

1 pear

1 apple

1 grapefruit

1 orange

1 mango

50 ml maple syrup

30 g butter

Boil the homards between two planks so that they do not bend while cooking. Remove the shell from the homards, salt and pepper the tail, and place in a casserole dish. Lightly sprinkle on oil, then place vanilla bean and lindenbaum leaves on top and roast in the oven.

For garnish, cut the accompanying fruits into bite-size pieces. Caramelize the fruits in a frying pan with the maple syrup and butter.

Cocotte of Bacon and Country-Style Cabbage

Phillipe Batton

A dish created by the expatriate French chef Phillipe Batton, during a battle versus Sakai using bacon.

This unassuming dish of cabbage, potatoes, mushrooms, and bacon cooked in a pressure cooker surprised the judges of the Gourmet Academy: the bacon that positively melts in your mouth, the savory vegetables that had soaked up the savor of bacon . . . This dish has made me reevaluate the essence of cooking, which is the relationship between the ingredients. It was a pleasant change from the other dishes, many of which run too wild in their attempts at creativity.

1 cabbage

Salted water, as needed

12 petite onions

1 kg bacon

500 g girolle mushrooms

Butter, for sauteing

1 clove garlic

12 small potatoes

2 L fond de veau

100 g chopped parsley

Thyme, to taste

Salt and pepper, to taste

Bay leaf

Tie up the cabbage, boil in salted water. Boil the petite onions in a different pot, also in salted water.

Cut the bacon into cubes. Saute the girolle mushrooms in butter. In a pressure cooker, add all the ingredients with the exception of parsley and cook for about 30 minutes.

When the ingredients are cooked, place the bacon and vegetables onto a plate. Add salt and pepper to the remaining sauce in the pressure cooker. Pour the sauce over the bacon and sprinkle parsley on top.

Ayu and Watermelon Mousse

Chen Kenichi

This unique dish was created during Battle Ayu and is a fine example of Chen's wit and knowledge. The combination of ayu and watermelon, which at first glance is unique, is in actual fact quite logical. Ayu, a freshwater fish, feeds off the moss found at the bottom of the river and has a very distinct aroma, which is often likened to that of watermelon. Chen utilized this similarity by combining the two. He could have used oranges or eggplants instead of the watermelon, but I must say that the watermelon proved to be a better choice. This dish, as had Phillipe Batton's dish, reiterated the importance of harmony between ingredients.

1 kg ayu

300 g watermelon

200 cc milk

50 cc fresh cream

Salt, to taste

Sugar, to taste

Rid the ayu of its bones and organs. Take out the seeds from the watermelon. Mix the ayu and watermelon using a mixer.

Whisk the milk, fresh cream, salt, sugar, and the mixture of ayu and watermelon together in a bowl. Using an ice cream maker, cool and solidify the mixture. Once the mixture is solid, arrange on a plate and serve.

Yellowtail with Daikon Radish

Fumiaki Sato

During the battle with 100 million yen's worth of Aritayaki dishware, Sato created this dish. Yellowtail with daikon is a traditional Japanese dish, but this dish was atypical. This young chef placed whipped cream on top of the daikon. I was wary of tasting this dish at first but was pleasantly surprised. The soy sauce that had seeped into the daikon, coupled with the whipped cream, gave it a softer taste. It was creamy and, frankly, very good. This dish, while being traditional, was innovative, hinting of a new age in Japanese cuisine.

1.5 kg yellowtail

Ice water

2 big daikon radishes

Salad oil

1440 cc katsuo dashi

180 cc sake

3 tablespoons sugar

180 cc light soy sauce

5 new bamboo shoots

1 carrot

180 cc mirin

90 cc tamari soy sauce

500 cc fresh cream, whipped

1 big ginger chopped finely, lengthwise

Kinome

Cut the yellowtail into small pieces, saute over fire until the surface becomes white. Once it is white, place in ice water to cool.

Peel the daikon radishes, cut up into pieces, and saute in oil until they brown. Add the fish and daikon to a pot, cook with katsuo dashi and sake. When the dashi is reduced to half, add sugar, and reduce further. When it is again reduced to half, add a bit of the light soy sauce. Reduce to half again. Then add the rest of the light soy sauce.

Meanwhile, boil the bamboo shoots. Cut the carrot into flower shapes. Add to the pot. Once all the ingredients have been cooked, add mirin and tamari soy sauce.

Arrange them on a plate, add whipped cream, ginger, and kinome on top and serve.

Chinese Cabbage with Mustard

Sai Gyokubun

Revered as a god, and bearer of the license of "special chef" in China, Sai Gyokubun unveiled this dish during Battle Chinese Cabbage. Every member of the Gourmet Academy was stunned by its taste. This dish changed our perception of Chinese cabbages as an ingredient solely for stews and pickles. It demonstrated the infinite ways that it could be cooked.

I was afraid that Chinese cabbage might have been too simple an ingredient for such a great chef but am now happy to have chosen it. It takes a true genius to create such an artistic dish out of such an ordinary ingredient.

500 g Chinese cabbage

Water

150 g sugar

100 cc vinegar

Salt, to taste

50 g Japanese mustard

Wash the cabbage and cut into 5-cm pieces.

Briefly boil the cabbage in water. Immediately take out and rid it of any moisture.

Combine sugar, vinegar, salt, mustard, and the boiled cabbage on a tray; wrap it tightly. Refrigerate for 2 to 3 days before serving.

Roasted Duck Stuffed with Foie Gras
Dominique Corby

This specialty of the Tour D'Argent was arranged by Corby for Battle Foie Gras. The unique part about this dish is how he used the duck as a sort of vacuum cooker in order to bring out the full taste of the foie gras. It is said that the best ways to cook foie gras is over direct heat and in a vacuum. Colby, without using a vacuum cooker, managed to do so by stuffing the foie gras into the duck.

The foie gras was cooked to perfection. This dish used the flavor of the ingredients to its fullest.

1 foie gras

Salt and pepper to taste

2 salted grape leaves

1 baby duck

4 eggplants, thinly sliced

S A U C E

1 L ruby port

200 cc jus de truffe

1 L fond de veau

20 g butter

4 white asparagus

4 green asparagus

Melted butter

Salt and pepper the foie gras well; cover with grape leaves.

Stuff the foie gras into the duck; roast in the oven at 400° for about 30 minutes. While roasting, try to baste as often as possible. Remove the duck from the oven while the inside is still pink. Keep warm for about 1 hour, so that the remaining heat cooks the foie gras.

Salt and pepper the eggplant; grill until completely cooked.

Reduce the ruby port until it is candylike in texture, then add the jus de truffe. Reduce further, and add the fond de veau and butter at the end to adjust the taste.

Boil both kinds of asparagus. Place the duck and foie gras onto a plate. Add the asparagus with melted butter and eggplant on the side.

Homard Steamed with Seaweed

Hiroyuki Sakai

Sakai created this dish in a battle to determine the strongest Iron Chef. He fought against his fellow comrade Chen, with homards as the theme ingredient of the battle.

"All I did was steam the homards with the salt from the seaweed. I wanted people to see that that was enough to give it its taste and delightful aroma." As he said, there is nothing difficult to this dish, and yet it managed to bring the house down. Actor Tatso Umemiya hailed this dish to be "the only correct way to eat an homard." And the usually cynical Chai Ran, excited beyond reason, exclaimed that the "presentation was outstanding."

This dish, brimming with the essence of the ocean and warmed with heated stones has the power to give pleasure to the diner.

2 (30-cm-long) toshishiri konbu

Water

Several stones heated over open fire

200 g raw wakame seaweed

4 homards

1 kg clams

1 red chili pepper

20 white peppercorns

1 L bouillon

Salt and pepper, to taste

Place the konbu in water. Heat the stones until burning hot.

In a copper pot, place 1 konbu and 100 g of wakame seaweed. Wash the homards well and place on top of this with the clams. Add the red chili pepper and white pepper; cover with the rest of the konbu and seaweed. Pour the bouillon over this, and warm over low heat.

About 5 minutes before serving, add the hot stones into the pot and let it steam.

When it is steamed, remove the homards; arrange on a plate. Add salt and pepper to taste.

Ronkonkai Chicken à la Dragee

Alain Passart

The star French chef Alain Passart created this dish. Though he lost against Sakai, this dish is worthy to be referred to as an artistic creation.

While observing Passart at work in Kitchen Stadium, I came to the realization that for a chef, flames have a godlike power in that they can completely alter the outcome of a dish. In order to finish this dish, he cooked the chicken slowly over low heat for 40 minutes. It was the same at the battle in Arashiyama, Kyoto, when the intensity of the fire was the key to cooking foie gras. Fire breathes life into an ingredient. The use of fire reflects the philosophy of each chef.

1 Ronkonkai chicken

Salt and pepper, to taste

Butter, to taste

Oil, to taste

4 beets

Salted water

50 g black olives

Dragee

Clean the chicken and add salt and pepper. Add butter and oil to the pot and warm over low heat. Add the chicken and brown slowly while basting.

Cut the beets into bite-size pieces and boil in salted water.

Remove the seeds from the olives and mince them. Combine with the beets to be used on the side.

Caramelize the dragee over heat and cool. Grind into tiny pieces and sprinkle over the chicken.

These 10 dishes will undoubtedly transform the culinary world in this century. Unfortunately, there were other dishes that could not be included this time. It is my hope that these 10 dishes will bring pleasure to your table.

In conclusion, I would like to give a big round of applause to the Iron Chefs, as well as the challenger chefs for a job well done. Working in an unfamiliar kitchen, with unfamiliar ingredients, and the time limit must have made the task unbearably difficult. Thank you so much for the wonderful work that you have all done.

THE IRON CHEF

Yutaka Ishinabe
(First Iron Chef French)

Way before the program actually began, Mr. Kyouichi Tanaka (the Director), asked me if I would be interested in taking part in a program where chefs battled with one another. I replied that while it would certainly be an interesting program for the producers and the viewers, it would be quite intense for the chefs. I asked him why he wanted to keep ragging on the chefs so much. Anyhow, I turned down his offer. A while later, though, I suggested that perhaps the program should take on a different perspective; perhaps it should be a program where the chefs won't merely be competing with one another, but a program where a new culinary discovery could be made. I never dreamed that this program would become such a big hit.

In the end, I decided to participate in this program not only because it sounded like fun but because I felt that I could make some contribution to the culinary world. All the existing cooking programs merely teach the viewer how to prepare a dish, and we, as chefs, learn nothing new from them. I figured that by creating an atmosphere where chefs were forced into creating an innovative dish, there would be more progress in the culinary world.

Honestly speaking, I was surprised by the costumes that they made us wear. I didn't want to wear something that stood out so much. . . . I had my kids to think about. I was surprised also by the fact that Mr. Kaga was going to be the host. He is an actor of such high caliber . . .

I didn't want to wear the costumes. . . . I had my kids to think about.

I was the Iron Chef for a short period of time at the beginning of the program. Many people have commented to me on what a composed warrior I was. I may have looked composed, but in actual fact, the expression I wore was one of distress. Other chefs seemed to have had rehearsals before the actual taping, but I never had one. I had to decide on the menu once the battle commenced. So the look I had was one of deep contemplation. I heard that later they started to give out five hints about the theme ingredients before the battle, but they didn't do this while I was on the program. You can imagine how drained I was after every show.

At the beginning, you couldn't bring in your own knives, plates, or anything onto the show. But the knife that I used for the first show was terrible; I couldn't cut anything with it. During the first battle using salmon, I couldn't even skin the salmon! I told them that I couldn't be expected to cook anything decent with those knives, and after that, they let us bring in our own knives.

After a while, they lifted the ban on bringing in our own plates. This was thanks to Mr. Michiba, who declared that the plates on the show were useless. They said that we could bring in our own plates until they bought a decent set for the show. But the more plates they bought, the more

dishes we had to prepare. They had so many rules at the beginning. They even banned us from using the oven.

Many people think that all these bans were my doing. This isn't entirely true. What I had in mind when I advised the production staff was that we should use utensils and ingredients that could be found in every household. We could be extravagant maybe once out of every three times. I thought that it would be more interesting if the chefs used staple items of every kitchen and whipped up a gourmet dish using them.

I continued thinking about this even after retiring from the show. I felt that the *Iron Chef* lacked a particular scenario. For example, "a date for two," "a banquet for an international summit," or "dinner for guests who came to the opening of a new airport." I wanted a theme for every episode. This dream was never realized. Well, they did have several, like Christmas, Valentine's Day, or Hanami (Cherry Blossom Viewing party), but I would have liked to see more of these.

I started feeling this way due to all the questions that I faced from the viewers. I received questions such as, "Why in the world did you pre-pare that fresh abalone like that? The freshness was lost." And, "How dare he spoil my precious abalone? It was meant to be eaten raw!" Our reasons for the way we used the ingredients were never clear to the viewers. If each episode had a theme, a particular situation, I thought that the view-ers would understand the reasons. This dish was prepared for such and such a theme, for this particular situation, and it wasn't done mindlessly. I really think that a themed episode would have made things more inter-esting for the producers, chefs, and viewers.

Anyhow, the program was a hit, it grew bigger, the dishes became more lav-ish. It affected the viewers in many ways. In good ways and bad, the *Iron Chef* left its mark on the Japanese society.

For example, when you go out to the countryside, you anticipate a delicious dish of boiled fresh vegetables cooked by the local ladies. Instead, you get a strange combination of ingredients served in the so-called *Iron Chef* style. When faced with such situations, I feel that the *Iron Chef* has done malice to society. We can't deny the fact that some of the dishes prepared on the program were a strange combination of ingre-dients.

On the other hand, we succeeded in showing that it was a worth-while program to appear on. At the beginning, this program was ridiculed within the culinary world. But as the program became a serious hit, a lot of chefs clamored for the opportunity to become a challenger. I have heard that the president of a major hotel prodded his chef to go on the show as a challenger. Such a phenomenon must surely be a first for culinary programs.

However, one has to experience it firsthand to understand how draining the show is. Coming from the school of belief that "Any experience is a worthwhile experience," I agreed to be on the show without much thought. Many chefs mistakenly think that it is easy, and that they would easily win that battle. If you ever try cooking under a time limit of an hour in your own kitchen, you will see that it is quite a difficult task.

Many of the challengers seemed to have practiced several times before going on the show. A chef with whom I am acquainted did so, too. I was surprised at how much practice he had put in. Many things could be said about the *Iron Chef,* but one thing that is clear is that all the chefs were serious about the whole enterprise.

At the beginning, you couldn't even bring your own knives.

It's interesting how a chef's personality is reflected under these trying conditions. The last battle, Alain Passart versus Hiroyuki Sakai was interesting in this way. It is my favorite battle.

The theme of the battle was Ronkonkai chicken. Mr. Passart cooked three whole birds. Though the end result looked the same, they were all cooked differently. One was steamed with hay, the other was roasted, and the third was poached. All three were, in fact, very different dishes. It was rural, yet urban, and it tasted very French and posh. It was classic, yet arranged in a modern manner, à la Passart. His personality was truly reflected in these dishes, and I was deeply moved.

I have an idea for an ultimate program. It would involve amassing as much money as possible, holding a preliminary battle in as many different countries, and bringing the victors someplace, such as Tokyo, for a final battle. The final battle would be held in a restaurant with seating capacity of about 40. There would be 40 judges. And 20 of these judges would be ordinary viewers who would have paid 20,000 yen (about $180)

for a ticket. The price is fair when you take into account that they will be feasting on gourmet dishes. Another 10 judges would be the program's sponsors and such, and the rest would be professionals in the culinary field.

The chef who is deemed to be victorious by these 40 judges will be awarded a monetary prize of about 30,000,000 yen (about $270,000). With this amount, a novice chef will have enough to open his own restaurant, and if he were Russian or Polish, there would still be enough to buy a house. In this way, there would be a good representation of truly skilled chefs, regardless of their fame. Wouldn't this be an interesting idea?

BATTLES 1 TO 50

Show No.	Japanese Air Date	Challenger	Iron Chef	Battle	Judges
1	10/10/93	Go Maruyama	Ishinabe	Salmon	Tamio Kageyama, Mitsuko Ishii, Masaaki Hirano
2	10/17/93	Yousei Kobayagawa	Michiba	Foie Gras	Yasushi Akimoto, Mitsuko Ishii, Asako Kishi
3	10/31/93	Indragoli Paulo	Chen	Blowfish	Tamio Kageyama, Mitsuko Ishii, Masaaki Hirano
4	11/7/93	Toshiyuki Kudo	Ishinabe	Tofu	Tamio Kageyama, Emi Inoue, Masaaki Hirano
5	11/14/93	Tomiteru Shu	Michiba	Homard	Tamio Kageyama, Emi Inoue, Asako Kishi
6	11/21/93	Kazuhiko Tei	Chen	Octopus	Yasushi Akimoto, Yoko Asaji, Masaaki Hirano
7	11/28/93	Masato Muto	Ishinabe	Daikon Radish	Yasushi Akimoto, Yoko Asaji, Masaaki Hirano
8	12/5/93	Tomitoku Shu	Michiba	Taraba Crab	Kiyohiko, Naeko Ishii, Masaaki Hirano
9	12/12/93	Eizou Ooyama	Ishinabe	Banana	Yasushi Akimoto, Minako Imada, Asako Kishi
10	12/19/93	Jacques Borie	Ishinabe	Chicken	Yasushi Tanaka, Mai Kitajima, Masaaki Hirano
11	1/9/94	Tomitoku Shu	Michiba	Pork	Shinichiro Kurimoto, Masaaki Hirano, Mariko Fuji

Show No.	Japanese Air Date	Challenger	Iron Chef	Battle	Judges
12	1/16/94	Wang Weiping	Chen	Squid	Yasushi Akimoto, Asaji Yoko, Masaaki Hirano
13	1/23/94	Jyun Hoshino	Michiba	Egg	Kiyohiko, Mitsuko Ishii, Masaaki Hirano
14	1/30/94	Toshio Tanabe	Michiba	Sea Bream	Yuuji Kamiashi, Mistuko Ishii, Asako Kishi
15	2/6/94	Kouichi Taniguchi	Chen	Shrimp	Tamio Kageyama, Mai Kitajima, Masaaki Hirano
16	2/13/94	Kazuyoshi Masaki	Michiba	Conger	Shinichiro Kurimoto, Masaaki Hirano, Mai Kitajima
17	2/20/94	Toshirou Kandagawa	Chen	Turbot	Katsuya Nomura, Mai Kitajima, Masaaki Hirano
18	2/27/94	Guy Shokr	Sakai	Oyster	Shinichiro Kurimoto, Masaaki Hirano, Mai Kitajima
19	3/6/94	Shinji Kondo	Chen	Flour	Tamio Kageyama, Masaaki Hirano, Yuriko Ishida
20	3/13/94	Hiroyuki Kitami	Sakai	Tomato	Tamio Kageyama, Mai Kitajima, Massaki Hirano
21	3/20/94	Kyouo Kagata	Chen	Scallop	Yuuji Kamiashi, Asako Kishi, Yuriko Ishida
22	3/27/94	Hideaki Odakura	Michiba	Cheese	Kiyohiko, Mai Kitajima, Masaaki Hirano

Show No.	Japanese Air Date	Challenger	Iron Chef	Battle	Judges
23	4/8/94	Koichiro Goto	Michiba	Rice	Yasushi Akimoto, Hikari Ishida, Masaaki Hirano
24	4/15/94	Munetaka Takahashi	Chen	Bamboo Shoot	Tamio Kageyama, Mayuko Takada, Masaaki Hirano
25	4/22/94	Mario Nakagawa	Sakai	Mutton	Tamio Kageyama, Mayuko Takada, Asako Kishi
26	4/29/94	Yukio Hattori	Michiba	Truffle	Joel Robuchon, Mai Kitajima, Masaaki Hirano
27	5/6/94	Hiromi Yamada	Chen	Cabbage	Shinichiro Kurimoto, Masaaki Hirano, Mayuko Takada
28	5/13/94	Hiromi Funatsu	Sakai	Skipjack	Daijiro Hashimoto, Mai Kitajima, Masacaki Hirano
29	5/20/94	Masatoshi Kimura	Sakai	Domestic Duck	Yasushi Akimoto, Mayuko Takada, Massaki Hirano
30	5/27/94	Kiyoshi Takahashi	Chen	Carrot	Yasushi Akimoto, Mayuko Takada, Masaaki Hirano
31	6/3/94	Kuniyuki Ishikawa	Michiba	Natto	Tamio Kageyama, Ritsuko Tanaka, Masaaki Hirano
32	6/10/94	Katsumi Hanato	Michiba	Ayu	Shigesato Itoi, Keiko Kono, Masaaki Hirano
33	6/17/94	Yuuji Wakiya	Sakai	Uni	Tamio Kageyama, Mayuko Takada, Masaaki Hirano
34	6/24/94	Masahiko Miyamoto	Chen	Milk	Kazuyu Okuyama, Mayuko Takada, Masaaki Hirano

Show No.	Japanese Air Date	Challenger	Iron Chef	Battle	Judges
35	7/1/94	Kouichi Tahata	Chen	Eggplant	Toshio Yamaguchi, Mayuko Takada, Masaaki Hirano
36	7/8/94	Takashi Mera	Michiba	Tuna	Shinichiro Kurimoto, Mayuko Takada, Asako Kishi
37	7/15/94	Tadkaaki Shimizu	Sakai	Homard	Shinichiro Kurimoto, Shyoko Tamura, Masaaki Hirano
38	7/22/94	Joel Bruant, Masashi Furutaka	Michiba, Chen	Sea Bass	Shinichiro Kurimoto, Mayuko Takada, Masaaki Hirano, Kazuko Kato
39	7/29/94	Mitsuru Saito	Sakai	Beef	Yasushi Akimoto, Nene Otsuka, Masaaki Hirano
40	8/5/94	Yasuhiko Yoshida	Michiba	Eel	Tamio Kageyama, Mayuko Takada, Masaaki Hirano
41	8/12/94	Hirohisa Koyama	Sakai	Hamo	Shigesato Itoi, Mayuko Takada, Masaaki Hirano
42	8/19/94	Keiji Nakazawa	Michiba	Corn	Yasushi Akimoto, Masaaki Hirano, Julie Dreyfuss
43	8/26/94	Katuyo Kobayashi	Chen	Potato	Shinichiro Kurimoto, Mayuko Takada, Masaaki Hirano
44	9/2/94	Hideki Oosako	Chen	Mushroom	Sakuji Yoshimura, Mayuko Takada, Masaaki Hirano
45	9/9/94	Artur Rütter	Michiba	Green Pepper	Shigesato Itoi, Kazuko Kato, Masaaki Hirano

Show No.	Japanese Air Date	Challenger	Iron Chef	Battle	Judges
46	9/16/94	Tsutomu Hiroi	Michiba	Saury	Tatsuo Umemiya, Mayuko Takada, Asako Kishi
47	9/23/94	Soutetsu Fujii	Sakai	Yam	Tamio Kageyama, Mayuko Takada, Asako Kishi
48	9/30/94	Takashi Saito	Chen	Shiba Shrimp	Tamio Kageyama, Mayuko Takada, Asako Kishi
49	10/7/94	Masamitsu Takahashi	Sakai	Matsutake Mushroom	Sakuji Yoshimura, Renho, Asako Kishi
50	10/14/94	Hoi Roi Wing	Michiba	Shark's Fin	Shigesato Itoi, Ryuuichi Sakamoto, Asako Kishi

TESTIMONY OF THE CAST AND STAFF

Bruce Seidel

(Director, Program Planning, The Food Network)

Before I came to work at The Food Network, there was a definite buzz within the television marketplace about *Iron Chef*. People were talking about this crazy show, but no one had ever seen it. So, it really didn't surprise me when one of my first assignments at the network was to view a few episodes of the series and render an opinion on the viability of the program for an American audience. I popped in the tape and was immediately mesmerized by Kaga's dramatic flare and the allure of the action unfolding within Kitchen Stadium. Although I did not completely under-

stand the Japanese commentary, the sports-style pageantry was certainly larger than life. I had never seen anything like it before.

Initially I was not sure if a mainstream audience would have an interest in *Iron Chef.* There has never been anything like it in food television. I thought it was similar to an old syndicated show called *Gladiators,* only with food. But there was something about the show's intensity; it was over the top and it pushed the envelope. There was a small group of us at The Food Network who thought it could work, and gradually we convinced the Powers That Be that we should take the risk and try *Iron Chef.*

Once we decided to take the brave step and put *Iron Chef* on the air, we set out to work with Fuji Television to prepare the episodes for an American audience. We dealt with technical issues: the length of the program, how Fuji would reedit the episodes to fit within our network clock parameters, and the best way to dub the commentary into English. The issue of subtitling took careful deliberation, as normally subtitles are not very commonplace within the U.S. Originally we had intended to dub Kaga's voice, but after seeing a completed show, we felt that the unique substance of the series would be missing. Eventually it was decided with Fuji to subtitle Kaga. The Fuji organization was extremely helpful in working within our needs and created a fantastic program for the American television viewer.

Instantly upon the Food Network launch of *Iron Chef* in July of 1999, people began talking. We were thrilled, but I must say that we all had a sense of unease about whether our audience was ready for such a show. Not only were they ready, but they have made *Iron Chef* one of the most popular shows on the network. Within a few weeks, we knew we had a hit on our hands.

The first I had heard about the possibility of the New York Battle was in January of 2000. We had a meeting with our Fuji contacts who

brought up the notion of a potential battle. Little did we know that it was going to take place in two months. We jumped at the chance to be involved and knew that the fans and viewers of *Iron Chef* would go wild. The next two months of my life were a complete blur. There were a ton of meetings, as well as hundreds of faxes and E-mails written to get the production aspects in order to satisfy the requirements of The Food Network. The logistics involved in this endeavor became a monumental effort.

I was involved in getting various talent on board and negotiating deals with these individuals, as well as negotiating our deal with Fuji, in order to give us the right to air the program on our network. The Food Network talent included our star chef Bobby Flay (*FoodNation*), Donna Hanover (*In Food Today*) and Gordon Elliott (*Door Knock Dinners*). These individuals all jumped at the chance to be involved, but I do not think anyone was aware of the roller coaster we were about to embark upon to make everything happen for the March taping. It was an exciting time, but hectic to say the least. In addition, it was a monumental effort to organize our publicity, press, on-air promotion, and sales teams to get the word out. Kaga and the Iron Chefs along with a thirty-plus person production crew were about to take over Manhattan.

Or were they?

Kaga is one of the top celebrities in Japan, and his schedule is very demanding. His time is very limited. In addition, because of his super celebrity status, his talent fee was not cheap. Since the New York Battle came together so quickly, and we were not sure of the press interest in the story, we didn't know if Kaga would be coming to the U.S. But the press interest in all things *Iron Chef* and Kaga was overwhelming. We decided to make the investment and have Kaga come to New York. It was definitely worth it.

The press went wild, from *Sports Illustrated* to *Entertainment Weekly* to *Newsweek* to the *New York Times,* and even a segment on *ABC World News Tonight* and *CNN Showbiz.* Oh, did I forget to mention *Vanity Fair* and *GQ?*

Many of the details of the battle sorted themselves out, but everything seemed to come together seconds before the battle was to be taped. None of us knew what the secret ingredient was going to be or if Kaga was going to be able to make it to New York or not. The taping finally got underway. It was a long evening, with some minor incidents, but the minute that Kaga walked into the New York battle stadium, we knew we had a hit on our hands. New York Battle earned The Food Network its highest rating to date.

Allez Cuisine!

TESTIMONY OF THE CAST AND STAFF

Osamu Kanemitsu

(Director, BS Fuji Programming and Production Department)

This program was a result of orders given to me by my boss, Mr. Yoshiaki Yamada, who said, "I want you to air a culinary program on Sunday nights at 10:30." It's only now that one can find culinary programs aired during the golden hours (7:00 to 11:00 P.M.), but back then, we never dreamed of airing one in this time slot. Culinary programs were aired during the lunch hours or in the afternoons, primarily for the housewives. It was unheard of to create a culinary program that was entertaining and one that could earn ratings as well. But I guess Mr. Yamada felt that culinary programs would be the next hit. Without his orders, this show would never have been born.

> Someone from the fire department had to be present during taping.

An ordinary culinary program decides on the recipes beforehand, and the program consists of showing the process of preparation. I wanted to get out of that mold, and do something totally different. I said, "Let's create a culinary program where the menu isn't decided on in advance." The concept behind the program was to "create a culinary program where the menu hasn't been decided on in an atmosphere like the Harrod's food emporium."

When I saw the unappetizing green Chinese dumplings during the first or second preliminary match, I thought that my idea might have been mistaken. We should do away with preliminary matches. Plus the ratings were awful. . . . No one had guessed correctly that this show would last this long.

We had our share of no-show challengers. Because they weren't actors, they didn't have managers or agents. Mr. Matsuo, the Producer, must have gone through a lot in this regard. Hana-chan [Assistant Producer Hanako Aso] negotiated relentlessly with the chefs and often-times had to con them into coming.

Many people voiced doubts about this program, saying that there wouldn't be enough challengers who would be willing to appear on the show. It was likely that the challengers would be defeated, and no one wants to be humiliated on national television. It was all due to Mr. Matsuo's gift as a producer that he was able to keep bringing new challengers.

Another struggle we had on the set was the lack of thermal power. Those portable gas ranges that we had were low on thermal calorie. We had requests for a specific calorific power. When we negotiated with the

personnel department of Fuji Television, they agreed to install a gas out-let in the studio. We had to extend the gas outlet into Studio 6 in the old corporate building in Kawadacho, for a mere 30-minute program. We had the support of the whole network, and I am truly thankful for that. Because of the fire regulations, someone from the fire department was also present during taping. That was the term of the deal. We also had to apply for the use of the gas outlet every time. For these reasons, the show had to be taped in this particular studio every time.

The *Iron Chef* requires a lot of enthusiasm, and that we were able to keep it up for so long was amazing. The energy and excitement was still there for the last episode. Programs, when they have been running for a while, start to get old and enthusiasm starts to dwindle. Things start becoming repetitive. But not for the *Iron Chef*. The energy was there throughout, and the last episode was incredible; we all felt that the show had enough energy to last for another 20 years. It's rare for a program to be able to exude so much excitement to the viewers.

I grew up watching American TV shows in Japan; and due to the admiration I had for these shows, I joined the TV industry. So when we were nominated for the American Emmy Awards, and the media from the States came to interview us, it was a dream come true for me. What more could a man wish for?

Yukio Hattori's Prestige Menu

For the compilation of this book, the complete history of the *Iron Chef,* I was requested by the Host to "choose the best dishes cooked in Kitchen Stadium, categorize them, and create the ultimate menu according to genre."

It was hard work to select the best menus out of all the wonderful dishes cooked in the past six years. To make it easier, I made a suggestion to the Host. I suggested that we choose a theme for each genre and create a menu according to that certain theme. The Host readily agreed to my suggestion, and thus the "Yukio Hattori's Prestige Menu" was created.

The courses that I have created in the following pages are what I felt would be suitable for this century. It is my wish that these menus will help enhance the enjoyment of food for everyone.

French Course

Until recent years, French food in Japan was merely an imitation of the true thing. But these days, traditional Japanese ingredients have been integrated, creating a style unique to Japan. With this new movement in mind, I have chosen dishes that are different from the traditional French dishes. In the eyes of classical French cuisine, these dishes are newcomers. I feel, however, that these dishes have the potential to become classic. Please enjoy the classic French course of the twenty-first century.

Hamo with Truffle Sauce Royale (Battle 41, Hamo)

The traditional royale dish arranged in a new manner by the use of hamo. The ingredient repeats itself in the fourth dish of hamo salad, but since I know how big a fan the Host is of this dish, I have decided to include it.

Homard Stuffed in Beets à la *Iron Chef* (Battle 127: Homard)

Iron Chef Sakai used the best homard from Britanny for this dish. He used the beet as a bowl and stuffed the homard into it. A sauce made of katsuo dashi and white miso was poured over it. The traditional Japanese sauce and flavors increases the homard's tastiness.

Chocolate-Flavored Tuna Cooked in Red Wine Sauce (Battle 249: Tuna)

I think the red wine from Château Montis would go very well with this dish. It is said that the accompanying wine should be similar to the one that was cooked with. In this way, both the wine and the dish will reach its full potential. A synergy will be created, transforming every mouthful into a piece of heaven.

Salad of Hamo and Prawns (Battle 41: Hamo)

It is known that a beautiful presentation is more appetizing, and this dish does just that. This dish is perfect after the heavy tuna, increasing one's anticipation for the next dish.

Roasted Pear with White Chocolate Orange Flavor
(Battle 118: Chocolate Pear)

Fruits cooked in liquor is a true classic. However, this dish is unique in that the peel is fried and used as a garnish, and pepper is sprinkled on top.

Harami of Lamb and Red Pepper Sorbet
(Battle 279: Lamb)

The rich saute of harami is eaten together with the sorbet. Sorbet and meats are usually not paired together in France. This dish was born in order to combat the aversion of the Japanese to fatty meats.

IRON CHEF

Iron Chef Interview

Rokusaburo Michiba

(First Iron Chef Japanese)

Mr. Matsuo and Mr. Tanaka came up to me one day saying, "We've got a new project; would you be interested?" That, I think, was the beginning of my involvement. I replied that the idea sounded interesting. I think they told me it would run for about six months, and I remember thinking that 6 months would be doable.

My impression when I first saw Kitchen Stadium? It was, "Wow!" I didn't like the outfit, though, but I was flattered into wearing it.

Initially, there were many conflicts with Mr. Matsuo and Mr. Tanaka. Being a TV show, I suppose a certain amount of performance is called for, but they wanted me to yell at my assistants or say things that would provoke the challengers. Also, when a younger chef designated me as the opponent, they were to yell out "Michiba," without a "Mr." or "Chef." I refused such rudeness. I told them that this went against the code of honor among the chefs. I went up to the challengers and told them that, "Look, life is long. When someone tells you to be rude, it's okay to refuse."

I really don't think that serious mindedness alone can make one an Iron Chef. You need to have a bit of actor in you. Both Mr. Sakai and Mr. Chen had that in abundance, and I was the sort of kid that when the teacher asked, "Who wants to be in the play?" I would be the first to yell, "Me!"

My impression when I first saw Kitchen Stadium? Wow!

Obviously, it was all serious business during the battles. I've had many people from the culinary world ask me, "Isn't it tough to finish everything in an hour?" There is never a second to spare, and all the while I am working on something, I am constantly thinking about the whole product. Even when I am walking around the streets, I am always making up themes, whether it be with tomatoes, carrots, or mackerel; and I practice making up menus in my head. I was always good with time allocation, but it got even better since I became an Iron Chef.

There was a battle using foie gras, which surprised all those who saw it. They were surprised that I was able to use it for a Japanese dish. The dish that I created, Kanpon, was a rearrangement of a dish I used to make when I was the chief chef of a Japanese restaurant in Akasaka. That dish had been prepared using the liver of an angler. For me, it was a dish that came about naturally.

I had always been a bit of a rebel in the world of Japanese cuisine.

My cooking was referred to as "Japanese cuisine à la Michiba." People snubbed my cooking, saying that my cooking wasn't "authentic" Japanese. In Japanese cooking, there is a set code, a set menu, for every season. For example, it's bamboo shoots and seaweed cooked in rice in the spring, grilled salted sweetfish in the summer, sea eels in late summer, steamed sea eels and matsutake in autumn. . . . It was too boring for me, doing the same thing year in and year out.

In Japan we say that in cooking, there are "five tastes, five senses," meaning that there is an infinite variety of tastes and textures of ingredients; however, once the ingredients are chosen, the taste and feel is chosen as well. If it's sea bream, it's sea bream; if it's tuna, it's tuna all the way, and there's no changing its basic taste or its basic texture. Even before I became an Iron Chef, I was always anxious to utilize different types of ingredients, such as shark's fin, the stomach of a shark, or a swallow's nest . . . ingredients that aren't used in Japanese cooking, ingredients that possess different characteristics from Japanese ingredients. Therefore I welcomed the idea of using new types of ingredients on the show.

> **Even when I am walking around the streets, I am always making up themes.**

I guess I'm different from other people. I have many friends who are chefs of different culinary venues. I think it's so much more interesting this way. You can never win against a Chinese chef when it comes to the restoration of dried foods. There is more of an exchange in ideas when you drink with chefs specializing in different foods.

Other than good time allocation, there were other things that I watched out for in Kitchen Stadium. First, creativity. Doing things in a

nontraditional way, so that the viewers can see that there are other ways of doing things. Second, maintaining elegance. The food obviously has to taste good, but I felt that a good presentation that can move a person was just as important. Third, I included at least one dish that a layman could prepare. I wanted the viewers to think, "I can prepare that too." I felt that people would tire of a program that always prepared intricate dishes. Perhaps I should have been a TV producer as well. . . .

All of the battles that I fought in Kitchen Stadium were memorable. I gave every one of those battles my very best. Winning or losing against chefs of a different genre was never important to me, but I could not bear to lose against a fellow Japanese chef. I was a rebel as well as a heretic in the Japanese culinary circle.

One must keep in mind that things are different from the old days. Better means of transportation means that you can get certain foods faster. Even from overseas, good ingredients are flown in every day. If a certain ingredient is good, I will use it regardless of where it comes from, or the season. That to me is the logical way to proceed. If Rikyu were alive today, I am sure that he would have done the same thing.

> **Winning or losing against chefs of a different genre was never important to me, but I could not bear to lose against a fellow Japanese chef.**

Looking at the young chefs, I think that Japanese chefs use the knife too much. They even use it to peel asparagus. I keep telling them to use a peeler. Just because you don't use the knife doesn't mean that you're a bad chef. It takes three times as long to peel a yamato potato when you use the knife, and a lot of it becomes wasted as well.

I was born during the war, so I don't like to waste things. I will use every usable bit of an ingredient. Take a fish, for example. I am constantly thinking of how I can use the skin, the organs, everything. You'd be surprised by how tasty the organs of a saury and sardine are.

Thus no theme can ever unnerve me. I ask myself, What is the essence of this ingredient? How can I best utilize it? At the end of the day, maximizing an ingredient's potential is the most important thing.

Battle Green Pepper is memorable in this regard. Adhering to the Japanese tradition of beauty, I let myself become obsessed with the presentation of the dish. Because of this, I lost against Mr. Rutter's dynamic dish. Just because a dish looks pretty doesn't mean that it moves you. Great cooking is when you can inspire someone with its taste. Even though I lost that battle, it was a turning point in my career as an Iron Chef.

The biggest enemy within Kitchen Stadium is not the opponent, but yourself. First of all, in this world, the basic jobs are done by the rookies. The younger ones do menial tasks such as filleting a fish or peeling a daikon. Having been out of touch with these tasks, it was tough for me when such skills were necessary for certain theme ingredients on the show.

> **The biggest enemy within Kitchen Stadium is not the opponent but yourself.**

Compared to when I was younger, my movements are not as quick or nimble. My strength has also weakened considerably. Before, I was able to crack open the skull of a sea bream, but now I need the help of a cutting board to do so. I used to be able to skin a turbot in one go, but now I have to take a breather in between. You know what they say; it's a sign of old age when you start saying "heave-ho!" before every move.

I retired from my role as Iron Chef for precisely these reasons. You have no business being on screen once you start heave-hoing. People thought that I was cool and collected, but no, my movements were just slow.

The definition of an Iron Chef? In China, there is an old word called *mokkei*. A king, who was very fond of chicken fighting, went out to seek the best fighter. But one chicken was too cowardly, the next too flighty, the next one too proud, having won too many battles. He could never find the right chicken. At the end, the best chicken was the one carved out of wood. Whether the opponent was a tiger or a lion, the wooden chicken was never agitated. Obviously, the reason is because it's made of wood, and it has no heart and, therefore, no feelings. So the moral of the story is that those who can fight without a "heart" win. The same goes for an Iron Chef. A strong Iron Chef is one who can keep his mind and soul focused on only the task at hand.

As for me, I was nearly 63 years old when they first offered me a position on the show. I was getting bored with my restaurant, and I was semiretired. I have a tendency to tire of projects once they start going well. I work night and day until the foundation is laid, and then I let someone else take over. I suppose I am like Ryuma Sakamoto or Shinsaku Takasugi of the Meiji Restoration. Like them, I am good at laying the foundation. Not like Hirobumi Ito, who took over and ran the country afterward.

No theme can ever unnerve me.

The *Iron Chef* rekindled in me an enthusiasm that I did not expect to feel at this age. Finding a battlefield restored in me a feeling of pleasant tension. If it weren't for the *Iron Chef,* I would have been retired, drinking sake everyday; perhaps I may have been dead by now. This program gave me something to be excited about for the last time. I still thank God for giving me this opportunity.

BATTLES 51 TO 101

Show No.	Japanese Air Date	Challenger	Iron Chef	Battle	Judges
51	10/21/94	Katsuyuki Sekihata	Sakai	Bread	Kenji Sawada, Mayuko Takada, Asako Kishi
52	10/28/94	Kouji Kobayashi	Chen	Pumpkin	Shinichiro Kurimoto, Eriko Kusuda, Asako Kishi
53	11/4/94	Yasuo Kawada	Michiba	Angler	Shinichiro Kurimoto, Mayuko Takada, Asako Kishi
54	11/11/94	Tadashi Sugita	Chen	Shanghai Crab	Tamio Kageyama, Mayuko Takada, Asako Kishi
55	11/18/94	Tatsuo Umemiya	Michiba	Mackerel	Shinichiro Kurimoto, Hisako Manda, Asako Kishi
56	11/25/94	Seiya Kawasaki	Sakai	Quail	Shinichiro Kurimoto, Hisako Manda, Asako Kishi
57	12/2/94	Toshikatsu Nakagawa	Chen	Noodle	Tamio Kageyama, Mayuko Takada, Asako Kishi
58	12/9/94	Furushyou Hiroshi	Michiba	Turkey	Tamio Kageyama, Mayuko Takada, Asako Kishi
59	12/16/94	Masayo Waki	Sakai	Strawberry	Yasushi Akimoto, Eri Fukazawa, Mayuko Takada, Asako Kishi
60	1/2/95	Toshirou Kandagawa	Michiba	Yellowtail (1995 Mr. Iron Chef Battle)	Koji Ishizaka, Mayuka Takada, Ryutaro Hashimoto, Asako Kishi

Show No.	Japanese Air Date	Challenger	Iron Chef	Battle	Judges
61	1/6/95	Toshiyuki Nakagawa	Chen	Mochi	Shinichiro Kurimoto, Akiho Chiho, Asako Kishi
62	1/13/95	Kouji Yamada	Sakai	Beet	Shinchiro Kurimoto, Mayuko Takada, Asako Kishi
63	1/20/95	Hisao Odachi	Chen	Chinese Cabbage	Tamio Kageyama, Mikiko Minami, Asako Kishi
64	1/27/95	Fuyuko Kondo	Sakai	Chocolate Apple	Yasushi Akimoto, Anna Umemiya, Asako Kishi
65	2/3/95	Yoshie Tobe	Chen	Soy Bean	Shinichiro Kurimoto, Mayuko Takada, Asako Kishi
66	2/10/95	Masuo Suzuki	Michiba	Matsuba Crab	Tamio Kageyama, Mayuko Takada, Asako Kishi
67	2/17/95	Kunio Hashimoto	Chen	Taro Potato	Tamio Kageyama, Mayuko Takada, Masaaki Hirano
68	2/24/95	Toshihiro Komine	Sakai	Asparagus	Tamio Kageyama, Tsurutaro Kataoka, Asako Kishi
69	3/3/95	Zeityen Wan	Michiba	Egg	Machi Tawara, Mayuko Takada, Shinichiro Kurimoto
70	3/10/95	Tetsutoshi Shimazu	Chen	Squid	Shinichiro Kurimoto, Asako Kishi, Kazuko Kato
71	3/17/95	Shigeo Yuasa	Sakai	Codfish	Shinichiro Kurimoto, Yasuko Matsuyuki, Masaaki Hirano

Show No.	Japanese Air Date	Challenger	Iron Chef	Battle	Judges
72	3/31/95	Liang Weiji	Chen	Pork (Hong Kong Battle)	Yuko Asano, Asako Kishi, Wu Jiali, Chai Ran
73	3/31/95	Shyu Chyu	Michiba	Ise Shrimp (Hong Kong Battle)	Yuko Asano, Asako Kishi, Jackie Chen, Chai Ran
74	4/7/95	Chiyo Cho	Chen	Tofu	Tamio Kageyama, Sachiko Kobayashi, Asako Kishi
75	4/14/95	Noriyuki Sawaguchi	Ishinabe	Flatfish	Shinichiro Kurimoto, Mayuko Takada, Asako Kishi
76	4/21/95	Kunio Santo	Sakai	Clam	Tamio Kageyama, Hisako Manda, Asako Kishi
77	4/28/95	Keisuke Tamano	Michiba	Amadai	Shinichiro Kurimoto, Chizuru Azuma, Asako Kishi
78	5/5/95	Myungsook Lee	Chen	Liver	Tsurutaro Kataoka, Mayuko Takada, Asako Kishi
79	5/12/95	Isao Yanagidate	Sakai	Caviar	Tamio Kageyama, Mayuko Takada, Asako Kishi
80	5/19/95	Elio Orsara	Chen	Kajiki Tuna	Tamio Kageyama, Yoko Shimada, Asako Kishi
81	5/26/95	Etsuo Jou	Michiba	Broccoli	Toshiki Kaifu, Sachiyo Kaifu, Mayuko Takada, Yasushi Akimoto
82	6/2/95	Katsuo Oomiya	Sakai	Onion	Shinichiro Kurimoto, Chizuru Azuma, Masaaki Hirano

Show No.	Japanese Air Date	Challenger	Iron Chef	Battle	Judges
83	6/9/95	Kazutaka Okabe	Sakai	Lamb	Tamio Kageyama, Chizuru Azuma, Masaaki Hirano
84	6/16/95	Meisei Sou	Michiba	Watari Crab	Shinichiro Kurimoto, Chizuru Azuma, Asako Kishi
85	6/23/95	Yukihiro Noda	Chen	Sardine	Hashinosuke Nakamura, Shinichiro Kurimoto, Hiroko Mita, Asako Kishi
86	6/30/95	Takayoshi Kamatani	Ishinabe	Avocado	Shinichiro Kurimoto, Chizuru Azuma, Asako Kishi
87	7/7/95	Takayoshi Kawai	Sakai	Turbot	Tamio Kageyama, Eriko Kusuda, Asako Kishi
88	7/14/95	Haruyoshi Omino	Sakai	Sweet Fish	Shinichiro Kurimoto, Mayuko Takada, Asako Kishi
89	7/21/95	Li Jinlun	Chen	Swallow's Nest	Shinichiro Kurimoto, Asako Kishi
90	7/28/95	Shinichi Nagamatsu	Sakai	Eggplant	Tamio Kageyama, Mayuko Takada, Asako Kishi
91	8/4/95	Toshimasa Hirano	Chen	Sea Urchin	Osamu Nishikawa, Eriko Kusuda, Asako Kishi
92	8/11/95	Kenji Kaji	Michiba	Umeboshi	Shinichiro Kurimoto, Mayuko Takada, Asako Kishi
93	8/18/95	The Salvatore Brothers	Michiba, Sakai	Tomatoes	Yasushi Akimoto, Hideki Saijo, Asako Kishi

Show No.	Japanese Air Date	Challenger	Iron Chef	Battle	Judges
94	8/25/95	Yoshiko Tamaki	Chen	Littleneck Clam	Nagisa Ooshima, Mayuko Takada, Asako Kishi
95	9/1/95	Joel Bruant	Sakai	Salmon	Shinichiro Kurimoto, Pinko Izumi, Asako Kishi
96	9/8/95	Minoru Noda	Michiba	Matsutake	Junichi Ishida, Mayuko Takada, Asako Kishi
97	9/15/95	Phillip Aubron	Sakai	Crawfish	Yasushi Akimoto, Taro Kimura, Asako Kishi
98	9/22/95	Tsuguo Fujiwara	Chen	Namako	Shinichiro Kurimoto, Chizuru Azuma, Asako Kishi
99	10/6/95	Hsu Cheng	Michiba	Squid (1995 Iron Chef World Cup)	Taro Kimura, Asako Kishi, Chai Ren, Julie Dreyfuss, Giorgio Lindo
100	10/6/95	Gianfranco Vissani	Pierre Gagnaire	Tuna (1995 Iron Chef World Cup)	Taro Kimura, Asako Kishi, Chai Ren, Julie Dreyfuss, Giorgio Lindo
101	10/6/95	Gianfranco Vissani	Michiba	Duck (1995 Iron Chef World Cup)	Koji Ishizaka, Anju Suzuki, Chai Ren, Toshiki Kaifu, Julie Dreyfuss, Giorgio Lindo

TESTIMONY OF THE CAST AND STAFF

Takashi Ishihara

**(Programming and Production Department, Drama Section, Fuji
Television)**

I saw the whole program happen in front of my eyes. My role in the history of *Iron Chef* is one of a witness.

The only opinion that I offered was one that I made during a meeting before the program formed its shape. My opinion was, "Wouldn't it be interesting if, let's say, a cabbage was placed on an elevator-like platform and brought up on stage?" That's all. Oh, and one more. There were many contenders for the role of Host, but I said, "Don't you think Mr. Takeshi Kaga would be perfect for the role?"

Culinary programs have been in existence since the advent of televisions. But their style has changed little over the years. There has been an increase in programs introducing new restaurants,

Wouldn't it be interesting if, let's say, a cabbage was placed on an elevator-like platform and brought up on stage?

but culinary programs were still saying things like, "add a pinch of salt here," "after 30 minutes in the oven, it will look like this," and so on. Then, Mr. Yoshiaki Yamada, the Director of the Programming and Production Department at Fuji Television, said, "Can't we do something about those culinary programs? Let's try something new."

At about the same time, Mr. Kyouichi Tanaka came up to me with an outline for a two-hour program with Kitchen Stadium. I can still clearly envision the diagram today. It was an image illustration of the set. Written with pencil in small letters was the title "The Iron Chef of Ovens." I thought it was a great idea, and I wanted to see it happen.

We flew to the United States and found a strange sight awaiting us. The Americans watching the program kept laughing.

Due to the wonderful timing, I decided to combine these two ideas, and we discussed them over and over. Fuji Television wanted a new type of culinary program. Mr. Tanaka dreamed of Kitchen Stadium. Luckily, these two ideas meshed.

We didn't realize it at the start, but just looking at the cooking process is enough enter-

tainment. Baseball and soccer, for example, do very much the same thing. I suppose it wasn't such a far-fetched idea to air a cooking program like a sports program. But even with these thoughts, we still had our doubts. Would we be able to keep the viewers' attention with 30 minutes of pure cooking?

For the first 2 months,

the ratings were in the single digits. Mr. Kanemitsu called for a meeting and said, "We need a change of direction. We will do away with preliminary battles. It will be a pure battle between the challenger and the Iron Chef. End of discussion."

We flew to the United States after we were honored with an Emmy nomination and found a strange sight awaiting us. The Americans watching the program kept laughing throughout our program. This sight reminded me of something. When the *Iron Chef* first began, it was something of a parody. For me, the elaborate set, the outrageous outfits that Mr. Kaga wore, were all a kind of mockery of the Michelin type of culinary establishment. The New Yorkers understood that concept.

Ironically, by the time we had gotten the Emmy nomination, the *Iron Chef* had become too much of a culinary authority. It had gotten too big and important, an establishment in its own right. The chefs who had declined to be on the show before now clamored for the chance, and being on the show had become a status symbol.

As a TV program, it was truly successful.

There were many battles, but my favorite one was with Mr. Alain Passart. Not that I know him personally, but the way he cooked that foie gras to perfection moved me to tears. He did it with his bare hands. . . . I kept wondering if it wasn't hot. He handled the foie gras like a precious infant, ever so carefully. We say that Japanese workmen love their tools, but I suppose there's a similarity here. It really moved me.

He turned the foie gras as if he were touching a fragile glass object that could break any moment. He showed me a truly unforgettable scene.

IRON CHEF

Yukio Hattori's Prestige Menu

Japanese Course

The theme I chose for the Japanese course is "A menu reflecting the change of season from winter to spring." But there is also another theme to this course. I feel that Japanese dishes these days do not always arouse one's appetite. I have therefore chosen dishes that "strongly stimulate the appetite."

Wakame Seaweed with Amber (Battle 175: Wakame Seaweed)

In a course menu, a certain equation is needed. Summed up in a single word, it is the importance of maintaining a balance. A stream of strong, aggressive dishes does not result in a satisfying course. While many of the dishes on the *Iron Chef* come on strong, this dish is a pleasant change in that it is subtle. One feels reenergized, ready to tackle the next course, after eating this dish.

Tuna and Leek Stew, Shabu Shabu–Style (Battle 220: Tuna)

The second dish is a soup, consisting of tuna balls and pieces of tuna. Piping hot soup is poured over the tuna, and it is eaten in the shabu shabu–style. Winter is the best season for tuna, and eating it warm on a cold winter's day enhances its flavor.

Fried Stuffed Lotus Roots (Battle 107: Lotus Root)

I chose this dish thinking that something crunchy was in order at this point. Fried stuffed lotus roots is a classic dish, but here, the Iron Chef stuffed it with prawns and truffles.

The Dynamic Cheese Hotpot (Battle 22: Cheese)

One dreams of a steaming hotpot on a cold winter's night. This is a dish that will surely warm you right up. Taraba crabs and clams are cooked in a steaming pot of katsuo dashi, white miso, and cheese. This dynamic dish will increase your appetite. Miso and cheese, at first glance a strange combination, go well together since they are both fermented products.

Gourmet Bowl of Foie Gras and Avocados (Battle 86: Avocado)

To end, a supreme dish created by Mr. Ishinabe. Avocados are usually eaten with soy sauce and wasabi, but here, it is paired with the fatty foie gras, creating a dish that has a very strong impact.

IRON CHEF

Chen Kenichi

(Iron Chef Chinese)

When I first heard about the concept of this show, I thought to myself, There are people in this world who come up with such strange ideas. It was another thing entirely when they asked me to become an Iron Chef. I agonized over whether to take the offer or not. There are chefs who declare that they are "the best chef in the world," but I was hardly that type. I am just like the person you see on TV, going around in the kitchen saying, "I wonder if this will turn out fine."

      If it were only myself that I was cooking for, I am confident that I would be able to cook something superb; but that is only because I know what I like. It's different when you are cooking for other people. My father taught me over and over again that customers have different tastes.

In a restaurant, we need to please the guests, to try to cook something that matches their taste. I want each and every one of my customers to go home feeling happy. But that program, the *Iron Chef,* doesn't reveal the ingredients until that moment, won't tell you who the judges will be either. So you don't know what you're working with, what kind of tastes the judges have, and then you get judged at the end. I didn't have the confidence to go through with that in the beginning.

Anyhow, I ended up taking their offer, thinking that humans need a constant challenge to break out of their shells in order to progress. I'm really a lazy person at heart. I need to be given a motivation to get going. Otherwise, I just let things pass me by. I felt that it would give me an opportunity to broaden my world, by handling different ingredients and dishes.

When I first heard about the concept of this show, I thought, There are people who come up with such strange ideas.

When I first became an Iron Chef, there was a lot of negative reaction regarding my decision. People would say things like, "What is that guy thinking?" But there were those who supported me and complimented me for being on a "good show." I guess things like that happen all the time. These words didn't bother me in the least. What I did was justified because I had a policy of my own. I wanted to make my restaurant better, and wanted more people to come. It's okay to be different, to not conform to society. So even though there was a pervasive atmosphere of slander and abuse, I never regretted my decision to be on the show.

There is no denying that TV has a strong influence, both good and bad. I had to be very careful of the image that I projected, because I knew that many were out to judge me according to what they saw. As the program got bigger, many more jobs came my way. I knew that I had to give every job my best if I wanted to maintain my reputation.

Up until then, I had made it a point not to delegate tasks to someone else, but to do them myself. I wanted my sweat and toil to be what made my customers happy. For example, if some regional hotel invited me to do a dinner show, I readily went. I would kill myself flinging the woks around, trying to please everybody. What made me happiest was when the people at the dinner show said to me, "Please come again." I love hearing these three words, "Please come again." So I put all of my effort into smiling and cooking the best dishes for my customers.

Ever since I became an Iron Chef, I realized even more the importance of every job and every encounter with a new person. Viewers of the program will say what they wish, and so it makes a job well done even more important.

> **I realized the importance of giving every job my best.**

There was a time when I decided to quit being on the show. I think it was about 3 years ago. My restaurant had been booked every single night ever since the show, and I didn't think that it was right of me to be away so often at this busy time. So I asked the Producer, Mr. Matsuo, if I could quit. Then all the staff members, and people like Mr. Sakai, called me and urged me not to quit.

If they had simply said "sure" when I told them that I wanted to quit, it would have ended at that. But when they said "No, you have to rethink it," I felt that I was truly needed. It's important for people to be in a situation where they are needed. At the end, Mr. Sakai and I had a heart

to heart. Mr. Sakai said, "Look, if you're going to quit, I will too. But if you aren't, let's give it our best together." He also added, "Whenever you have a problem, talk to me. I will help you in every way that I know." In the end, we promised each other to give it our very best.

After talking to Mr. Sakai, I realized that quitting the show wasn't the solution. I needed to be on it in order to enjoy myself. After this realization, I stayed on for the whole 6 years.

Around the middle of the 6 years, the level of the challengers became much higher, and the judges demanded more from us. Because the show had been airing for so long, the challengers came well prepared. They brought with them their special recipes. We needed to constantly come up with something new.

When I said, "I want to quit being on the show," everyone begged me to rethink it. At that moment I truly felt needed.

If I knew who the judges were beforehand, I could be more prepared. There were usually four judges on the *Iron Chef*. On the battlefield, you cook according to your style and belief. But there were times when you adjusted your dishes according to the judges. We got five hints before the show, and I thought of possible menus then. I may have decided to prepare A but, after seeing who the judges were, changed to B. It's a bit of a gamble really. When I succeeded in guessing the judges' tastes, I usually won.

I kept changing my menus during the battle. I would have a basic idea, but I played around with it and kept adding new ideas to it. I think my assistants had a hard time keeping up with me. Usually, after receiving the five hints, chefs would sit down with their assistants and discuss what they would make for each ingredient. They would write down the recipes and everything. I never had a recipe prepared. I was Mr. Capricious, Mr. Whimsical Chen.

But on the other hand, I

think my assistants were constantly aware that we were a team. Some of my assistants were truly amazing. I would ask them if they could deal with sea urchins, and they would say yes and work away. And they would be better than me. I used to tease them about them being the real Iron Chefs.

As I said during the final taping of the show, nothing about me has changed since I became an Iron Chef. I still do things the same way, and I still act the same way toward others. And I will remain this way forever. But one thing that must change with the passing of the years is my skills as a chef. This means that I will have to continue going to different places, seeing and tasting many different things. Then I need to create new dishes from these experiences. If you don't put into practice what you've seen, you'll never become better. This is especially true for cooking. I am constantly going to different places for new discoveries, but I tend to mix pleasure with business.

My assistants had a hard time. I was Mr. Capricious, Mr. Whimsical Chen.

This attitude is due to my mother's upbringing and my father's attitude to business. My father was really serious about his work. He was very driven and worked hard to provide us children with everything our hearts desired. Seeing my father's attitude led me to feel that I must work hard, and play hard.

These 6 years have been truly enjoyable for me. I got to meet many new people, got to visit many new places. . . . It was such fun. I am so glad I stuck with it for 6 years.

I couldn't have done this without the support of my staff at my restaurant. Toward the end of the show, whenever I got hints for the next theme, the young chefs in my restaurant would think about possible new menus and bring me their new ideas. My staff has suffered through these 6 years with me. From now on, I want to concentrate on educating these young chefs. There are so many chefs with such great potential. It would be delightful if even one of them became a star of the culinary world.

BATTLES 102 TO 150

Show No.	Japanese Air Date	Challenger	Iron Chef	Battle	Judges
102	10/13/95	Sadaharu Nakajima	Sakai	Rice	Shinichiro Kurimoto, Mayu Tsuruta, Mayuko Takada, Asako Kishi
103	10/20/95	Kunbi Rin	Michiba	Potato	Nagisa Ooshima, Yoshiko Ishii, Mayuko Takada, Asako Kishi
104	10/27/95	Kunbi Rin	Michiba	Sweet Potato	Nagisa Ooshima, Yoshiko Ishii, Mayuko Takada, Asako Kishi
105	11/3/95	Masahiko Hagiwara	Chen	Tenaga Shrimp	Shinichiro Kurimoto, Mayuko Takada, Kazuko Kato, Asako Kishi
106	11/10/95	Kiyotaka Ikegawa	Chen	Crab	Nagisa Ooshima, Wakamatsu Oyakata, Mayuko Takada, Chai Ran
107	11/17/95	Toshirou Kandagawa	Sakai	Lotus Root	Tamio Kageyama, Sanshi Katsura, Julie Dreyfuss, Asako Kishi
108	11/24/95	Bruno Menard	Sakai	Escargot	Yusushi Akimoto, Keiko Saito, Jun Inoue, Asako Kishi
109	12/1/95	Shyozo Miyamoto	Chen	Carp	Shinichiro Kurimoto, Chizuru Azuma, Bessho, Asako Kishi
110	12/8/95	Tadamichi Ota	Sakai	Octopus	Shinichiro Kurimoto, Amon Miyamoto, Kazuko Kato, Asako Kishi

Show No.	Japanese Air Date	Challenger	Iron Chef	Battle	Judges
111	12/15/95	Phillip Groud	Sakai	Oyster	Yasushi Akimoto, Fumie Hosokawa, Julie Dreyfuss, Yoshiko Ishii
112	12/22/95	Chen	Sakai	Chicken (1995 Mr. Iron Chef)	Shinichiro Kurimoto, Tamio Kageyama, Maki Mizuno, Chai Ran, Asako Kishi
113	1/3/96	Chen	Michiba	Beef (1995 Mr. Iron Chef)	Katsuya Nomura, Yuko Asano, Nagisa Ooshima, Chai Ran, Asako Kishi
114	1/12/96	Gao Jinyi	Chen	Dried Abalone	Nagisa Ooshima, Judy Wong, Shinichiro Kurimoto, Yoshiko Ishii
115	1/19/96	Hidetoshi Ushimaru	Sakai	Curry Powder	Shinichiro Kurimoto, Keiko Saito, Sanshi Katsura, Asako Kishi
116	1/26/96	Hiroshi Yamanobe	Chen	Hogfish	Nagisa Ooshima, Chizuru Azuma, Ukyo Katayama, Asako Kishi
117	2/2/96	Yoji Watanabe	Chen	Terrapin	Shinichiro Kurimoto, Mayuko Takada, Hideki Takahashi, Asako Kishi
118	2/9/96	Tadashi Yanagi	Sakai	Chocolate Pear	Tamio Kageyama, Chizuru Azuma, Masahiko Kondo, Asako Kishi

Show No.	Japanese Air Date	Challenger	Iron Chef	Battle	Judges
119	2/16/96	Jinichi Tateyama	Sakai	Leek	Nagisa Ooshima, Keiko Saito, Kiyohiko, Asako Kishi
120	2/23/96	Takaya Nakazawa	Chen	Shiitake Mushroom	Tamio Kageyama, Judy Wong, Tsurutaro Kataoka, Asako Kishi
121	3/1/96	Kiyoshi Suzuki	Nakamura	Foie Gras	Shinichiro Kurimoto, Sachiyo Nomura, Ken Tanaka, Asako Kishi
122	3/8/96	Tatsujiro Yoshida	Chen	Codfish	Nagisa Ooshima, Chizuru Azuma, Hirofumi Banba, Asako Kishi
123	3/15/96	Senji Osada	Sakai	Scallop	Shinichiro Kurimoto, Eriko Kusuda, Masaki Kanda, Asako Kishi
124	3/22/96	Kunbi Rin	Nakamura	Green Pepper	Tamio Kageyama, Reiko Kato, Shigeaki Sayegusa, Asako Kishi
125	3/29/96	Katsuaki Mori	Chen	Spinach	Tamio Kageyama, Hiroko Mita, Sakuji Yoshimura, Asako Kishi
126	4/12/96	Bernard le Branse	Nakamura	Salmon (French Battle)	Yoko Shimada, Asako Kishi, Joel Robuchon
127	4/12/96	Pierre Gagnaire	Sakai	Homard (French Battle)	Pierre Troisgro
128	4/19/96	Toyoaki Suganuma	Nakamura	Egg	Shinichiro Kurimoto, Keiko Masuda, Kunio Murai, Asako Kishi

Show No.	Japanese Air Date	Challenger	Iron Chef	Battle	Judges
129	4/26/96	He Yiewen	Chen	Lettuce	Tamio Kageyama, Mayuko Takada, Kazuo Zaizu, Asako Kishi
130	5/3/96	Katsuko Nanao	Nakamura	Codfish Egg	Shinichiro Kurimoto, Bessho, Kazuko Kato, Asako Kishi
131	5/10/96	Shuji Morikawa	Chen	Pineapple	Tamio Kageyama, Iyo Matsumoto, Dave Ookubo, Asako Kishi
132	5/17/96	Tamotsu Takao	Sakai	Abalone	Tamio Kageyama, Keiko Saito, Yoshio Mori, Asako Kishi
133	5/24/96	Kenji Motai	Nakamura	Udon Noodle	Yasushi Akimoto, Sachiko Kobayashi, Tatsuo Umemiya, Asako Kishi
134	5/31/96	Ichio Goto	Chen	Aori Squid	Shinichiro Kurimoto, Mayuko Takada, Takenori Emoto, Asako Kishi
135	6/7/96	Yoshinobu Sonobe	Sakai	Ikura	Emoto, Hisako Manda, Yukio Hatoyama, Asako Kishi
136	6/14/96	Kangi Son	Nakamura	Skipjack	Shinichiro Kurimoto, Yutaka Enatsu, Hiroko Mita, Asako Kishi
137	6/21/96	Philippe Batton	Sakai	Bacon	Shinichiro Kurimoto, Chizuru Azuma, Masumi Okada, Asako Kishi

Show No.	Japanese Air Date	Challenger	Iron Chef	Battle	Judges
138	6/28/96	Hideo Tozawa	Nakamura	Clam	Yasushi Akimoto, Mayuko Takada, Teimei Kanou, Asako Kishi
139	7/5/96	Takayuki Nomura	Chen	Sweetfish	Shinichiro Kurimoto, Kaori Momoi, Tsurutaro Kataoka, Asako Kishi
140	7/12/96	Hideki Yamamoto	Nakamura	Sea Eel	Tamio Kageyama, Hideki Takahashi, Reiko Kato, Asako Kishi
141	7/19/96	Yoshimasa Uki	Sakai	Ootoro Tuna	Emoto, Mayuko Takada, Shingo Yamashiro, Asako Kishi
142	7/26/96	Masaru Toriumi	Nakamura	Iwa Oyster	Tamio Kageyama, Keiko Saito, Shingo Yamashiro, Asako Kishi
143	8/2/96	Takeshi Yamamoto	Chen	Black Pork	Tenmei Kano, Saya Takagi, Kunihiko Mitamura, Asako Kishi
144	8/9/96	Thierry Houngues	Nakamura	Caviar	Takenori Emoto, Keiko Saito, Tsurutaro Kataoka, Asako Kishi
145	8/16/96	Toshizo Tsugawa	Chen	Anago Eel	Tamio Kageyama, Tomoko Nakajima, Kenichi Tanizawa, Asako Kishi
146	8/23/96	Kenji Sugawara	Sakai	Corn	Tamio Kageyama, Chizuru Azuma, Ichiro Zaizu, Asako Kishi

Show No.	Japanese Air Date	Challenger	Iron Chef	Battle	Judges
147	8/30/96	Shinsuke Shimada	Chen	Taisho Prawn	Tamio Kageyama, Keiko Saito, Ichiro Zaizu, Asako Kishi
148	9/6/96	Takamasa Uetake	Nakamura	Peach	Tamio Kageyama, Akiko Yano, Tenmei Kano, Asako Kishi
149	9/13/96	Chomei Son	Sakai	Softshell Crab	Tamio Kageyama, Saya Takagi, Tadao Takashima, Asako Kishi
150	9/20/96	Tokuo Endo	Nakamura	Saury	Tamio Kageyama, Chizuru Azuma Tsurutaro Kataoka, Asako Kishi

Yukio Hattori's Prestige Menu

Chinese Course

I chose dishes from the hot Szechwan cuisine and the milder Cantonese cuisine in order to create a menu that played up these two contrasts. One must keep in mind the many different characteristics when choosing dishes for a course menu. Taste, smell, texture (the feel inside the mouth, the texture when you bite into it, and the way it goes down your throat) are all such characteristics. I created this menu to focus on mainly the taste of these dishes.

Papaya and Coconuts with Crab Sauce (Battle 174: Papaya)

This new type of Chinese dish, created by the chef of Japanese nouvelle Chinois, Mr. Yuiji Wakiya, is papaya heaped on Chinese spoons with a sauce made of coconut milk and crabs and baked. Your mouth is filled with the sweetness of papayas and coconuts with every mouthful.

**Shiba Shrimp with Chili Sauce Served on a Canapé
(Battle 48: Shiba Shrimp)**

In the twenty-first century, chili will become the rage all over the world. Keeping this in mind, I especially chose two Szechwan dishes both with chili in them. This dish is not as piquant because the chili sauce is made of eggs and ketchup.

Stir-Fried Squid and Shark's Fin (Battle 70: Squid)

This dish will soothe the inside of your mouth after a hot, spicy dish. This dish is created with a stir-fry of minced squid and meringue inside a shark's fin soup. It will surely reaffirm the tastiness of squids. The fluffy texture and sweetness will delight your palette.

Homard Gyoza Dumplings and Spicy Hotpot Stew
(Battle 296: Homard)

This is an extravagant dish, a stew made with the essence of homard spiced with red chili bean pastes and homard gyoza dumplings. The dumplings are put into the stew and it is eaten together. Such an extravagant dish could only have been created in Kitchen Stadium. For this reason, I have decided to include this dish in the menu. The dumplings made of minced pork meat and homard create a sweet taste that goes very well with the spiciness of the stew. The spiciness and sweetness create a depth to this dish.

Spicy Papaya Soup (Battle 174: Papaya)

This dish, declared to be addictive by the judges, is fitting as the last chapter to a delightful course. The aigyoku jelly eaten with the soup creates a unique blend of different spices.

IRON CHEF

Koumei Nakamura
(The Second Iron Chef Japanese)

I used to see Mr. Michiba at the golf course. At the time he was wondering if he should retire from the show or not, and every time he saw me, he would ask, "Koumei-san, would you like to become the next Iron Chef?"

But I kept saying, "I could never do that" and kept turning him down. I was only a hired chef back then. The choice of whether to be on the program or not was not mine. In the chefs' associations, there was a permeating belief that *"Iron Chef* is wrong, whatever they make on the program is not Japanese." So honestly, I didn't want anything to do with it.

When they officially asked me to be on the show, I remember calling my older brother in Kyushu and seeking his advice. He's not really my brother, but I met him when I was working at a greengrocer's while attending night high school. He was the son of the greengrocers. I said, "They want me to be on the *Iron Chef* but I don't know if I want to do it." He replied, "Look, no matter what anyone says about the matter, the fact is, there is only one Iron Chef for Japanese cuisine in the whole world. It's a big chance for you. Take it." These words were pretty much what made me decide.

I think that I was the Iron Chef most concerned about winning. Mr. Sakai and Mr. Chen always did their jobs in a very composed manner. Their mental power is amazing. I always felt pressured, feeling that I couldn't lose against them. The other Iron Chefs all owned their own restaurants and were free to cook whatever dish they felt like. But because I was hired at Nadaman, I didn't have as much freedom.

Mr. Sakai and Mr. Chen always did their jobs in a very composed manner. Their mental power is amazing. I always felt pressured.

At the time, I was the head chef of all 8 of the Nadaman restaurants, the department head of the culinary department, the director of the company and was also the director of the culinary research department. I juggled four titles, and with so many titles, I couldn't afford to be a loser. Whenever we received a hint about next week's theme, there would be a meeting within the company. We would then test a recipe and seek the chairman's advice.

The battle fought between Mr. Michiba and myself for the New Year's osechi wasn't really Michiba versus Nakamura. It was more a battle between Mr. Michiba and Nadaman. I'm sure Mr. Michiba had a tough time, but I had the whole organization to think about. In the beginning I was referred to as the "tactician," and that compounded the pressure even further.

Of course, there were dishes that I wanted to cook. I wanted to accomplish my beliefs as a chef, and I didn't want to lose. They say that as long as you do your best, winning shouldn't matter, but it did to me.

I really dreaded going home when I lost. My son, who was in junior high school, would tell me, "Dad, how come Rokusaburo Michiba never lost but you do? I don't want to go to school and face everyone tomorrow." That was harsh. My wife too, would tell me that she was too embarrassed to go out when I lost.

So after a year on the show, I bought a miniature Shiba dog. I needed one ally in the family. I named him "Chef" after *Iron Chef*. He has been unfailingly loyal to me since day one. He is my most trusted ally and friend. He is the only one who really understands me.

Halfway through, I came upon a major realization. Dishes that I usually cook at Nadaman will not help me win on the show. During the clam battle, I cooked a very orthodox dish. The judges proclaimed that it wasn't very *Iron Chef*. Not that the food at Nadaman is bad or anything.

It just means that traditional cuisine is not what they are looking for on the show. A new type of Japanese cuisine, a futuristic dish, needs to be created in order to win acclaim.

I decided after a while not to cook in the Nadaman style, but to bring out my personal style. I was most conscious of this during the battle with Mr. Kandagawa's apprentice, Battle Saury.

I dreaded going home when I lost. My son and wife would tell me they were too embarrassed to go out. That was harsh.

No one at the office said anything to me after about a year on the show. They seemed to have lost interest in winning every match. That made things a lot easier for me. At the last battle against Mr. Yukio Hattori, Battle Tuna, I was able to smile throughout. Ms. Kishi, who tasted my dish, told me, "You seem to be very relaxed today." A year later I was on the show as a challenger and fought against Mr. Morimoto in Battle Egg. I was really relaxed then. One needs to be relaxed to win on that show. Thinking back, I think I was too conscious of everyone around me. I constantly needed to please everyone. I wish that I had been myself more. This is a big regret for me.

All the ingredients for the battles that I fought were difficult ingredients. I suppose the viewers are entertained when they see me agonize over a non-Japanese ingredient, but it was hell for me. I often felt like crying. There were things like beef tongue and duck . . . yes, duck was hard. It's not the duck that we use in Japan. Rather, it was the type used in Europe. My opponent was Tour d'Argent's Mr. Leprin, a veritable guru of ducks. No way I could win. In Arashiyama, the theme was foie gras. I have never heard of a Japanese chef use these ingredients. At least then I tied against Mr. Passart.

I guess I became stronger when I took on a "come what may" attitude. After that, I won against Mr. Michiba, and I was victorious against Mr. Morimoto as well. I did pretty well in the key battles. It also meant, though, that I made silly mistakes after taking on this attitude.

I remember Battle Ostrich. That was a real headache. But because of this match, we were nominated for the Emmys.

Battle Pepper against Kunbi Rin was memorable. I stuffed green pepper noodles inside a yellow pepper and poured a red pepper sauce over it, creating a tricolored dish. It was perfect, the best dish I ever made on the show.

All the ingredients were difficult. I suppose the viewers were entertained. . . . I often felt like crying.

On the other hand, Battle Egg that I had against Toyoaki Suganuma, a French chef, was awful. I prepared a dish of steamed sankai fresh eggs. We were supposed to use quail's eggs, but I mistakenly used different types of eggs, including salmon roe and dried mullet roe. The taste was pretty bad. I knew when I tasted it that I had lost.

Battle Potato was memorable too. It was a tie, and there was a rematch two weeks later. I felt sorry for Mr. Kojima, who was my opponent. His performance that day was only a tenth of his usual performance due to unfortunate happenings and mistakes made by his assistants. Back in the waiting room, we consoled each other, saying that we would try harder next time. Oh, and Mr. Yonemura, with whom I had Battle Wakame Seaweed. That was a great battle as well. He was an incredible chef.

Anyhow, all the themes that were given to me were ingredients that were not used for Japanese cuisines. They were hard. If they had given me vegetables like matsutake mushrooms, bamboo shoots, or beets, I know I would've won, hands down.

I suppose, though, that these ingredients taught me a valuable lesson. Many chefs become clumsy on camera. So Mr. Matsuo and the other staff members had to learn new things in order to make the show better. The important thing is, one needs to constantly be willing to learn new things.

BATTLES 151 TO 200

Show No.	Japanese Air Date	Challenger	Iron Chef	Battle	Judges
151	10/4/96	Takeo Kashiwabara	Chen	Winter Melon	Tamio Kageyama, Kazuko Kato, Hideki Takahashi, Asako Kishi
152	10/11/96	Son, Sen	Syou, Chen	Chicken (Peking Battle)	Con Lee, Chai Ran, Shiji Tanimura, Yuki Saito, Asako Kishi
153	10/11/96	Son	Chen	Shark's Fin (Peking Battle)	Con Lee, Chai Ran, Shiji Tanimura, Yuki Saito, Asako Kishi
154	10/18/96	Fujita Shin	Nakamura	Soba	Tenmei Kano, Keiko Saito, Tabuchi Kouichi, Asako Kishi
155	10/25/96	Ryuichi Ogusu	Nakamura	Chestnut	Tamio Kageyama, Mayumi Asaka, Masumi Okada, Asako Kishi
156	11/1/96	Daniella Ozik	Chen	Mushroom	Shinichiro Kurimoto, Megumi Ooishi, Knihiko Mitamura, Yoshiko Ishii
157	11/8/96	Hiroshi Yamaoka	Sakai	Chinese Cabbage	Tamio Kageyama, Keiko Saito, Masumi Okada, Asako Kishi
158	11/15/96	Wayne Nishi	Sakai	Apples	Shinichiro Kurimoto, Mayuko Takada, Takenori Emoto, Yukio Hattori

Show No.	Japanese Air Date	Challenger	Iron Chef	Battle	Judges
159	11/22/96	Kenjiro Kuroki	Nakamura	Angler	Shinichiro Kurimoto, Nagisa Katahira, Tenmei Kanou, Asako Kishi
160	11/29/96	Kiyoshi Miyashiro	Nakamura	Beef Tongue	Tamio Kageyama, Megumi Ooishi, Takao Horiuchi, Asako Kishi
161	12/6/96	Yukio Ishizaki	Chen	Garlic	Takenori Emoto, Masaki, Kanda, Kazuko Kato, Asako Kishi
162	12/13/96	Yoshio Suzuki	Sakai	Orange	Shinichiro Kurimoto, Tenmei Kano, Toyama Kyoko, Yoshiko Ishii
163	12/20/96	Bernard Leprince	Nakamura	Duck	Shinichiro Kurimoto, Keiko Saito, Masumi Okada, Agathe Morechand, Jean Sylvestre
164	12/31/96	Koumei Nakamura	Michiba	Osechi (100 People Battle)	Mr. & Mrs. Hata, Mr. & Mrs. Ochiai, Mr. & Mrs. Umemiya, Mr. & Mrs. Matsumoto, Tamio Kageyama, Yuko Asano, Asako Kishi
165	1/10/97	Hiroshi Michifude	Chen	Dried Shell Ligament	Takenori Emoto, Megumi Oishi, Ichiro Zaitsu, Asako Kishi
166	1/17/97	Hiroshi Kasahara	Sakai	Mochi	Shinichiro Kurimoto, Nobuko Ochiai, Asako Kishi
167	1/24/97	Laurie Kennedy	Sakai	Unagi Eel	Tamio Kageyama, Yoko Saito, Masumi Okada, Asako Kishi

Show No.	Japanese Air Date	Challenger	Iron Chef	Battle	Judges
168	1/31/97	Laurie Kennedy	Sakai	Pigeon	Tamio Kageyama, Yoko Saito, Masumi Okada, Asako Kishi
169	2/7/97	Hiroyoshi Morie	Nakamura	Takaashi Crab	Shinichiro Kurimoto, Ichiro Zaitsu, Kazuko Kato, Asako Kishi
170	2/14/97	Houkou Koh	Chen	Rice	Tenmei Kanou, Asako Kishi, Keiko Saito, Akira Fuse
171	2/21/97	Tetsuo Shimada	Sakai	Truffle	Takenori Emoto, Keiko Masuda, Tsurutaro Kataoka, Asako Kishi
172	2/28/97	Tatsuo Yamazaki	Nakamura	Natto	Shinichiro Kurimoto, Toshio Shiba, Keiko Saito, Asako Kishi
173	3/7/97	Etsuo Jou	Sakai	Wine	Tamio Kageyama, Kazuko Kato, Kazuhiko Kato, Asako Kishi
174	3/14/97	Yuuji Wakiya	Chen	Papaya	Tamio Kageyama, Chizuru Azuma, Koutaro Satomi, Asako Kishi
175	3/21/97	Takashi Yoneyoshi	Nakamura	Wakame Seaweed	Shinichiro Kurimoto, Megumi Ooishi, Kinya Kitaoji, Asako Kishi
176	3/28/97	Hiroyuki Kitami	Sakai	Honey	Takenori Emoto, Yasuko Agawa, Kazuhiko Kato, Asako Kishi

Show No.	Japanese Air Date	Challenger	Iron Chef	Battle	Judges
177	4/11/97	Koukan You	Nakamura	Hanami (Cherry Blossom Viewing)	Shinichiro Kurimoto, Yuko Asano, Eiji Bando, Masumi Okada, Asako Kishi
S178	4/18/97	Shinzo Okumura	Sakai	Bamboo Shoot	Takenori Emoto, Hisako Manda, Ichiro Zaitsu, Asako Kishi
179	4/25/97	Chihiro Ootsuki	Chen	Tomato	Tenmei Kanou, Asako Kishi, Minako Honda, Tsurutaro Kataoka
180	5/2/97	Kiyoyasu Sasaki	Sakai	Sea Bass	Tenmei Kanou, Asako Kishi, Sayuri Ishikawa, Sanshi Katsura
181	5/9/97	Norio Higashiya	Nakamura	Pork	Shinichiro Kurimoto, Kayoko Kishimoto, Hideki Takahashi, Asako Kishi
182	5/16/97	Gillian Hearst	Nakamura	Ostrich	Shinichiro Kurimoto, Chizuru Azuma, Masaki Kanda, Asako Kishi
183	5/23/97	Masao Takagi	Chen	Pidan	Tenmei Kanou, Lisa Junna, Chai Ran, Joji Yamamoto
184	5/30/97	Germano Orsara	Sakai	Ham	Tamio Kageyama, Keiko Saito, Tatsuo Umemiya, Asako Kishi
185	6/6/97	Hisato Sakane	Nakamura	Anago Eel	Takenori Emoto, Reiko Takashima, Tsurutaro Kataoka, Asako Kishi

Show No.	Japanese Air Date	Challenger	Iron Chef	Battle	Judges
186	6/13/97	Masahiko Hagiwara	Kobe	Short Pasta	Shinichiro Kurimoto, Masumi Okada, Kazuko Kato, Asako Kishi
187	6/20/97	Kunio Sato	Sakai	Yellowtail	Shinichiro Kurimoto, Akiko Yano, Kunihiko Mitamura, Asako Kishi
188	6/27/97	Kenchu Shu	Chen	Aka Grouper	Tenmei Kanou, Saya Takagi, Chai Ran, Asako Kishi
189	7/4/97	Masami Shikajima	Nakamura	Prawn	Tamio Kageyama, Keiko Saito, Hideki Takahashi, Asako Kishi
190	7/11/97	Toshiyuki Ishikawa	Sakai	Sea Urchin	Takenori Emoto, Megumi Oishi, Yasosuke Bando, Asako Kishi
191	7/18/97	Yoshikazu Matsuno	Chen	Partridge	Shinichiro Kurimoto, Kayoko Kishimoto, Ichiro Zaitsu, Asako Kishi
192	7/25/97	Stephano Tabacci	Kobe	Cabbage	Tamio Kageyama, Hitomi Takahashi, Sunplaza Nakano, Asako Kishi
193	8/1/97	Seiji Toyoshima	Sakai	Milk	Takenori Emoto, Naomi Kawashima, Takao Horiuchi, Asako Kishi
194	8/8/97	Sakai, Kobe	Nakamura, Chen	Water-melon	Shinichiro Kurimoto, Keiko Saito, Tatuo Meidaka, Asako Kishi

Show No.	Japanese Air Date	Challenger	Iron Chef	Battle	Judges
195	8/15/97	Souseiko Kawaguchi	Chen	Eggplant	Tenmei Kanou, Harumi Inoue, Koutaro Satomi, Asako Kishi
196	8/22/97	Androsoni Pietro	Sakai	Melon	Kazuhiko Kato, Yoshiko Ishii, Tamio Kageyama, Sae Ishiki
197	8/29/97	Yoshinori Kojima	Nakamura	Potato	Tenmei Kanou, Senri Yamabuki, Tetsuya Bessho, Yoshiko Ishii
198	9/5/97	Yoshinori Kojima	Nakamura	Jyoka Flatfish	Tenmei Kanou, Hiroko Moriguchi, Gitan Ootsuru, Yoshiko Ishii
199	9/12/97	Toshiyuki Nakajima	Sakai	Beef Cheek	Kageyama Tamio, Kishimoto Kayoko, Okada Masumi, Kishi Asako
200	9/26/97	Miyuki Igarashi	Chen	Cucumber	Shinichiro Kurimoto, Toyama Kyoko, Tatsuo Meidaka, Asak Kishi

TESTIMONY OF THE CAST AND STAFF

Kyouichi Tanaka
(Director)

When Fuji Television asked me, "Could you create a culinary battle program, a program where contestants compete with their culinary skills?" I wondered how I could make such a program dramatic.

Initially, I thought of a program where we would have about five professional chefs lined up. We would have ordinary people challenge them. It would be like having these ordinary people venture into a strange world, a fictional world, which would be interesting to watch. The

professional chefs would be challenging them from above; it wouldn't be a battle on an equal basis. There would be a definite hierarchy involved. That's the first idea that I presented to them.

I asked the opinions of many in the culinary world, like Mr. Mitsugu Yuuki, and they pointed out a big problem to me. Mr. Yuuki said, "A battle between two different types of cuisine, like a battle between French and Japanese, wouldn't work. If you are going to go through with this idea, then I suggest that you have a judge who will judge the better dish according to his preference."

I agreed with Mr. Yuuki at first, but decided to go through with it anyway. We figured that it would be more interesting if there were many different types of cuisines. The timing was perfect, since at the time there was a movement in the culinary world where chefs were using different types of ingredients. Japanese chefs were incorporating ingredients like caviar, French chefs used shark's fin, and so on.

If this program had been created 2 or 3 years earlier, it wouldn't have worked since it would have been too avant-garde. Had it been 2 or 3 years later, this concept would have been too old. This concept of a "battle between differing cuisines" came at the right time.

A culinary program, as a genre, is something that pleases everyone and is easy to watch. Even if it is dramatized, the viewers can readily follow it. That is why we had a unique host like Mr. Takeshi Kaga and had the chefs wear strange costumes. So long as they are bonafide chefs, the program will work.

It seems that everyone hated the costumes. Mr. Rokusaburo Michiba especially did not look very good in them. Mr. Yutaka Ishinabe kept saying "No, no!" The costume for Mr. Chen Kenichi fit him so well that it was kind of funny. When we lined up Mr. Michiba, Mr. Ishinabe, and Mr. Chen for a panel photograph in the very beginning, I was secretly worried that it was a bad idea. It was my idea to dress them up like that, and it worried me.

For any program that is made, it is important that the program be convincing to both laymen and professionals. It's important that laymen

Everyone hated the costumes.

who have no knowledge of cooking be able to enjoy the program. We also wanted professionals to gain something from watching the show. Fortunately for me, I wasn't very interested in cooking, but I didn't dislike cooking either. Because I didn't feel strongly either way, it was easier for me to direct this show.

I must admit that chefs look good on film. No other business involves so much action. It's entertaining and cool.

Yukio Hattori's Prestige Menu

Italian Course

The key terms *health* and *nutrition* will be the most important aspects of food in the future. For this Italian course, unlike the other courses, I concentrated on these two notions when deciding on the dishes. Titled, "The Ideal Nutritious Energy Food," it includes proteins and sugar in abundance. Eaten one hour before any sports activity, it is sure to give you the necessary powers.

Carpaccio of Beef Tenderloin and Maitake Mushrooms
(Battle 256: Wild Maitake Mushroom)

These days there exists carpaccios made of fish, but traditionally they are made with thin slices of beef in sauce. In these terms, this is a true carpaccio. Beef has a lot of protein, which helps in the development of muscles. I recommend this dish to individuals who play sports.

Banana Pepporoncino (Battle 267: Chocolate Banana)

Instead of using bananas for desserts, this dish used them as a meal by downplaying the sweetness. Rich in sugar and potassium, bananas are quickly changed into energy. They also help in the contraction of muscles.

Pasta Made of Soba Wheat—Cabbage and Truffle Flavored (Battle 27: Cabbage)

This dish of fettuccini made of soba wheat, with truffles and prosciutto on top, is one of the best pasta dishes created on the *Iron Chef*. Its nutrition content is excellent as well; there is a lot of sugar in this dish, which means more energy before playing sports.

Fried Minced Calamari (Battle 48: Shiba Shrimp)

This dish draws its hint from the traditional Japanese cuisine of calamari balls and fried minced fish. By deep-frying the calamari, the sweet and fragrant nature of the calamari is enhanced. The crunchiness of the calamari is also pleasing.

Heart-Shaped Cocoa Ravioli (Battle 267: Chocolate Banana)

The dish chosen for dolce is the Cocoa Ravioli. Bananas and Gorgonzola cheese are wrapped inside chocolate-flavored ravioli, and deep-fried. The overpowering sweetness of the banana is kept in check by the bitterness of the cocoa. It is a dessert for a mature adult.

IRON CHEF

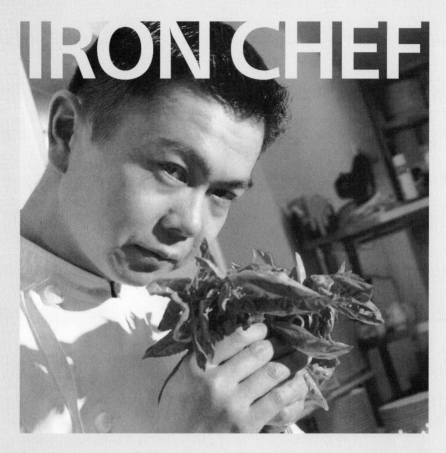

I r o n   C h e f   I n t e r v i e w

Katsuhiko Kobe
(Iron Chef Italian)

I was in Italy from February 1994 until April 1997. I was first enrolled in a hotel school for foreigners in Turin. After finishing there, I went on to work at the Enoteca Pinocchioli in Florence. About three months before finishing my apprenticeship there, the headmaster of the hotel school called me and said, "There is a culinary contest in Japan. Would you be interested?" I guess the headmaster didn't exactly know what this contest was. This contest turned out to be the *Iron Chef.*

At the time, the production staff was looking for a young chef to become an Iron Chef. They were conducting a search in Italy of Japanese chefs studying here. My name was on the list along with about 20 others. Mr. Matsuo, the producer, and Ms. Asao, the assistant producer, came to Torino to interview me. That was how it all happened.

At first I thought I was going to be a challenger. I had been watching the show before I left for Italy. Watching Mr. Michiba, Mr. Ishinabe, and Mr. Chen in action, I used to think, "I hope that I could become a chef like them in about 10 years." I never dreamed that I would become one of them.

I found out that I was an Iron Chef about 3 days before leaving for Japan. Several production staff members came to Italy saying that they wanted to make an introductory film on me in Italy. Talking to them, I sensed something was wrong. Mr. Matsuo said to me, "I hope this arrangement will work for a long while" and I thought, If I am only going to be on the show once, as a challenger, why is he saying these things to me? I figured out that I was actually an Iron Chef at the end of the taping. My mind was in a state of panic. The *Iron Chef* was an influential show, and one couldn't do just anything and get away with it. You couldn't edit things out like they do for other shows. I didn't want to do anything that would compromise the world of Italian cuisine. I was at a loss.

The *Iron Chef* was an influential show, and one couldn't do just anything and get away with it.

My worries were blown away when I saw the costume that I was to wear. I went to Fuji Television straight from Narita Airport, and there was my costume. I had come back from my apprenticeship wearing a ratty stadium jumper and sneakers, so the costume was a shock to me. It wasn't

reluctance I felt; it was more a feeling of resignation. I figured that I have to do what I have to do. Basically I don't like losing, and if I am going to do it, I wanted to do it well.

The factor that worried me most was time. Being a cook, it is a given that I produce something that tastes good. What made it difficult was the time constraint. You couldn't finish in 50 minutes, nor could you finish in 61 minutes. I always included one dish of pasta, so time became more of an issue for me.

Basically, anything can be made into a pasta dish. But it is impossible to do that in 1 hour, especially since my pasta was handmade. People may say, Then don't do pasta, but I think that pasta is important for Italian food, and I wanted the viewers to become familiar with many different types of pasta. So I made them, knowing that it would be practically impossible.

For the first battle with short pasta, I hadn't yet gotten a handle of the time, so I flopped it. If pasta isn't eaten immediately after it's cooked, it becomes soft and tastes completely different from when it is first made. The Iron Chef whose pasta is tasted later is in a bad position. When I realized this, I started to veer toward dishes such as gratin where timing isn't as crucial.

Because I was dealing with pasta, the time between the match and the tasting was a battle for me. I had to worry about time more than the other chefs did. For stewed dishes, it's to your advantage if your dish is tasted later, as the flavor has more time to settle. Sometimes I wished I were the "Prince of Stews" rather than the "Prince of Pasta."

Sometimes I wished I were the "Prince of Stews" rather than the "Prince of Pasta."

Yes, the start dash, that looks pretty meaningless, but it is in fact a very important time saver. During my first battle, I took my sweet time choosing my ingredients. After the taping, Mr. Matsuo said to me, "What was that start dash? Are you an old man or what?" I had been in the track and field team in high school and had confidence in my running abilities. So from the second battle, I ran around as fast as I could. I started the mad dash for these stupid reasons, but in truth, there are times when you are five seconds short to completion. It's at those times you wish that you had saved more time earlier. People often question me about what that start dash is all about, but there is a legitimate reason to it.

The battle that I remember most is my debut battle. I was really chagrined at that battle against Mr. Hagiwara. I would love to have a revenge match against him. Battle Chevreuil was also memorable. I can say this now that it's over, but I think that there were some battles which, though I may have lost, I still think I was better. The battle that I admit

my complete defeat was the battle against Mr. Fukatsu. His cooking was unbelievable.

The dishes that I am most proud of are the dishes I created during Battle Mango. Up until then, I had only used mangos in desserts, so I was really proud of them. They were pure perfection. The roasted duck, which was duck roasted with mango, was the best. Mango has the ability to soften meats. It goes well with bloody meats due to its slight acidity and fragrance. The best part of a duck is its skin, but if the duck is roasted with mangos, its skin will be ruined.

The Roasted Duck during Battle Mango, that was pure perfection.

So what I did was, I roasted the duck first, without the mango, and then added it. I stuffed more roasted mangos into the duck as well, in order to enhance its fragrance. The accompanying leek was stewed with mangos as well. I think this dish was well balanced.

The dishes created on the *Iron Chef* are so costly that they are usually not used in restaurants. But I did serve that mango duck once. Several neighborhood epicureans requested the dish, so I made it for them. I had to charge them 15,000 yen ($135) just for that dish. But epicureans are always eager to try different dishes, and since they were regular patrons, I served it to them. I heard that the patron was a fan of the show and went around boasting that he had eaten the roasted duck.

I was invited to lecture at many different schools since being on the show. A lot of the students saw me as a sort of goal. Mr. Michiba and Mr. Sakai, as well as Mr. Chen, are way up there. It would take forever to come even close to their league. I am more accessible, and I suppose the students look at me and think that if he can make it, so can I. I became an Iron Chef just 5 years after graduating from college. In some ways, I proved that hard work is the easiest way to realize a dream.

There are many students in culinary schools studying Italian cuisine. But once they start working and are faced with problems with other chefs, or they hit a slump, many of them quit. It would be impossible for people like them to ever become a Mr. Michiba or a Mr. Sakai.

I too have problems at work. But looking at me, they see their future in a shorter time frame. I'm a more attainable goal for them. I guess my being an Iron Chef had some meaning.

Mr. Michiba and Mr. Sakai, as well as Mr. Chen, are way up there. It would take forever to come even close to their league. I am more accessible.

My own goals? I am opening my own restaurant, so I would like to see it succeed. The name of the restaurant has already been decided on. It will be my Italian nickname, Massa.

My real nickname is "Masa," but when Italians pronounce it, it always comes out as "Massa." I decided to use the name I was called during my days in Italy. It's the first time I have my own restaurant, so I would welcome any support.

BATTLES 201 TO 250

Show No.	Japanese Air Date	Challenger	Iron Chef	Battle	Judges
201	10/3/97	Fujio Imai	Kobe	Matsutake	Tamio Kageyama, Tsurutaro Kataoka, Megumi Ooishi, Asako Kishi
202	10/10/97	Liu Xikun	Nakamura	Beef (1997 Iron Chef World Cup)	Kinya Kitaoji, Sae Isshiki, Chai Ran, Asako Kishi, Daniel Birman, Christian Boucharac
203	10/10/97	Peter Clark	Passard	Homard (1997 Iron Chef World Cup)	Kinya Kitaoji, Sae Isshiki, Chai Ran, Asako Kishi, Daniel Birman, Christian Boucharac
204	10/10/97	Alain Passart	Nakamura	Foie Gras (1997 Iron Chef World Cup)	Kinya Kitaoji, Sae Isshiki, Chai Ran, Asako Kishi, Daniel Birman, Christian Boucharac
205	10/17/97	Matsuo Nagasaka	Chen	Spare Rib	Shinichiro Kurimoto, Yoshizumi Ishihara, Keiko Saito, Asako Kishi
206	10/24/97	Masashi Goto	Sakai	Langoustine	Tamio Kageyama, Megumi Ooishi, Kazuhiko Kato, Chieko Honma
207	10/31/97	Yuji Seki	Kobe	Chestnut	Tenmei Kanou, Kazuko Kato, Koki Mitani, Chieko Honma
208	11/14/97	Keiji Azuma	Nakamura	Lamb	Shinichiro Kurimoto, Tokiko Kato, Ishihara, Asako Kishi

Show No.	Japanese Air Date	Challenger	Iron Chef	Battle	Judges
209	11/21/97	Toru Matsushima	Chen	Shanghai Crab	Shinichiro Kurimoto, Yoko Akino, Hideki Takahashi, Asako Kishi
210	11/28/97	Kazunari Takada	Kobe	Milt	Tenmei Kanou, Shiho Hashimoto, Kazushige Nagashima, Yoshiko Ishii
211	12/5/97	Kazunari Takada	Kobe	Botan Prawn	Tenmei Kanou, Shiho Hashimoto, Kazushige Nagashima, Yoshiko Ishii
212	12/12/97	Maurice Guillouet	Nakamura	Scallop	Tamio Kageyama, Kaori Momoi, Ryouichi Kawamura, Christian Boucharac
213	12/19/97	Yasumasa Takagi	Kobe	Strawberry	Tenmei Kanou, Naomi Hosokawa, Kazushige Nagashima, Asako Kishi
214	12/26/97	Toshio Kandagawa	Nakamura	Ara Fish	Shinichiro Kurimoto, Hiromi Iwasaki, Korn, Yoshiko Ishii
215	1/9/98	Akihiko Inoue	Chen	Aramaki Salmon	Shinichiro Kurimoto, Katsuya Nomura, Sachiyo Nomura, Asako Kishi
216	1/16/98	Yasuhiro Fukatsu	Kobe	Chevreuil	Yasushi Akimoto, Keiko Saito, Yoshizumi Ishihara, Asako Kishi

Show No.	Japanese Air Date	Challenger	Iron Chef	Battle	Judges
217	1/23/98	Yoshimasa Matsumoto	Sakai	Matsuba Crab	Shinichiro Kurimoto, Yoko Akino, Yutaka Enatsu, Yoshiko Ishii
218	1/30/98	Choki Tou	Chen	Blacktiger Prawns	Tamio Kageyama, Megumi Ooishi, Yoshizumi Ishihara, Chai Ran
219	2/6/98	Fumiaki Sato	Sakai	Daikon Radish	Shiichiro Kurimoto, Kotaro Satomi, Keiko Iiboshi, Kazuko Saiki
220	2/20/98	Yukio Hattori	Nakamura	Tuna	Shinichiro Kurimoto, Masumi Okada, Hisako Manda, Asako Kishi
221	2/27/98	Yukio Hirayama	Morimoto	Sea Bream	Yasushi Akimoto, Masumi Okada, Kaori Momoi, Asako Kishi
222	3/6/98	Motohito Kondo	Sakai	Hina Matsuri	Yumi Adachi, Naomi Hosokawa, Yoko Akino, Asako Kishi
223	3/13/98	Mario Frittoli	Kobe	Broccoli	Shinichiro Kurimoto, Chizuru Azuma, Yutaka Enatsu, Asako Kishi
224	4/3/98	Masayoshi Kimura	Morimoto	Rice	Tenmei Kanou, Yoko Akino, Hideki Saijyo, Asako Kishi
225	4/10/98	Tomoji Ichikawa	Sakai	Guinea Fowl	Shinichiro Kurimoto, Kuniko Asaki, Masumi Okada, Kazuko Saiki

Show No.	Japanese Air Date	Challenger	Iron Chef	Battle	Judges
226	4/17/98	Mitsurou Harada	Chen	Spanish Mackerel	Kazuhiko Kato, Chizuru Azuma, Takao Horiuchi, Asako Kishi
227	4/24/98	Takashi Shimamura	Chen	Hiragai	Tenmei Kanou, Keiko Saito, Yoshizumi Ishihara, Asako Kishi
228	5/1/98	Tetsuo Hagiwara	Morimoto	Bamboo Shoot	Tenmei Kanou, Kayoko Kishimoto, Ryugo Hashi, Asako Kishi
229	5/8/98	Masanobu Watanabe	Kobe	Mango	Tenmei Kanou, Mayuko Takada, Korn, Asako Kishi
230	5/15/98	Yasuhiko Habuchi	Morimoto	Asparagus	Shinichiro Kurimoto, Miwako Fujitani, Hideki Takahashi, Kazuko Saiki
231	5/22/98	Zyukyou Ryo	Chen	Pork Rib	Shinichiro Kurimoto, Keiko Saito, Yoshizumi Ishihara, Kazuko Saiki
232	5/29/98	Zyukyou Ryo	Chen	Konnyaku	Shinichiro Kurimoto, Keiko Saito, Yoshizumi Ishihara, Kazuko Saiki
233	6/5/98	Kumiko Kobayashi	Sakai	Mishima Beef	Tenmei Kanou, Megumi Oosihi, Korn, Kazuko Saiki
234	6/12/98	Keiichi Miyanaga	Morimoto	Sweetfish	Shinichiro Kurimoto, Sae Isshiki, Teruhiko Saigo, Asako Kishi

Show No.	Japanese Air Date	Challenger	Iron Chef	Battle	Judges
235	6/19/98	Kentaro	Chen	Baby Potato	Tenmei Kanou, Sachiko Kobayashi, Junichi Ishida, Asako Kishi
236	6/26/98	Yasuhiro Sasajima	Kobe	Kamo Eggplant	Shiichiro Kurimoto, Yoshizumi Ishihara, Kazuko Kato, Asako Kishi
237	7/3/98	Takaji Yoshida	Morimoto	Tofu	Shinichiro Kurimoto, Kuniko Asaki, Masumi Okada, Kazuko Saiki
238	7/10/98	Shuzo Shimokawa	Sakai	Manka Pork	Shinichiro Kurimoto, Keiko Masuda, Tsurutaro Kataoka, Asako Kishi
239	7/17/98	Junichi Ito	Chen	Yogurt	Shinichiro Kurimoto, Yoko Akino, Teruhiko Aoi, Yoshiko Ishii
240	7/24/98	Takeshi Kajimoto	Morimoto	Abalone	Tenmei Kanou, Hitomi Takahashi, Tsurutaro Kataoka, Asako Kishi
241	7/31/98	Miyoko Sakai	Kobe	Watarigani	Kanou Tenmei, Kayoko Kishimoto, Shuko Takeda, Kazuko Saiki
242	8/7/98	Hirokazu Handa	Morimoto	Big Eel	Shinichiro Kurimoto, Maiko Kawakami, Masaki Kanda, Asako Kishi

Show No.	Japanese Air Date	Challenger	Iron Chef	Battle	Judges
243	8/14/98	Masanobu Watanabe	Sakai	Peach	Shinichiro Kurimoto, Miwako Fujitani, Kazushige Nagashima, Kazuko Saiki
244	8/21/98	Kaoru Miyazawa	Chen	Carp	Tenmei Kanou, Maiko Kikuchi, Kinya Kitaoji, Asako Kishi
245	8/28/98	Sakai, Ishinabe, Jou	Chen, Waki, Miyamoto	Pork, Terrapin, Banana (Host's 2000 Plate Special Battle)	Shinichiro Kurimoto, Mitsuko Ishii, Kenji Fukui, Asako Kishi
246	9/11/98	Kyonori Miura	Sakai	Surume Squid	Tenmei Kanou, Fumie Hosokawa, Yoshizumi Ishihara, Kazuko Saiki
247	9/18/98	Hideki Maruyama	Chen	Sardine	Tenmei Kanou, Keiko Saito, Teruhiko Saigo, Kazuko Saiki
248	9/25/98	Shuichi Fujii	Morimoto	Keiji	Shinichiro Kurimoto, Kuniko Asaki, Masumi Okada, Asako Kishi
249	10/2/98	Shinya Tasaki	Kobe	Tuna	Shinichiro Kurimoto, Naomi Kawashima, Masumi Okada, Sakao Kishi
250	10/9/98	Ron Seigel	Sakai	Lobster	Tenmei Kanou, Aiko Morikawa, Kazuhiko Kato, Kazuko Saiki

TESTIMONY OF THE CAST AND STAFF

Kenji Fukui
(Announcer, Fuji Television)

This program is too demanding so I hope that it stays in an eternal sleep. If we must air this program, I can maybe handle it once every 6 months. The physical, emotional fatigue afterward is comparable to broadcasting a 3-hour marathon.

A request was made to the broadcasting department of Fuji Television for a sports broadcaster, who can broadcast a culinary compe-

tition. The first job that I had when I first joined the company was broadcasting a boxing match. There are several competitors involved in many sports, but boxing is done one on one. I thought that that style would be more suitable for the *Iron Chef*, so I said, "I can broadcast it in a boxing style." They told me, "Fine, then could you make it a real fighting event?" This is how I ended up broadcasting the show.

I didn't know a thing about cooking. I still don't. About the only thing that I can cook is instant noodles, so during the whole taping, I kept asking Mr. Hattori questions. I bombarded him with questions like, "What is mentori?" "What is vapeur?" "What is mise en place?" and "What is chao?"

This program is too demanding; I hope it is put in an eternal sleep.

To make it a real sports event style of broadcast, I should have enrolled in the Hattori Nutrition College for a month or so and learned a thing or two about cooking. That would have been the ideal, but I figured I didn't have to go that far. You know how there are certain dishes, let's say Italian dishes, that no matter how many times you ask questions about it, you still don't understand it. I was positive the viewers had the same questions as me, so I keep asking them. If I pretended to know what was going on, my character wouldn't come out, and I thought a totally specialized program wouldn't be fun to watch.

The show was broadcast in a 99 percent sports style, except that there are climaxes in sports events. For the *Iron Chef*, the whole hour is a climax. So I have to keep up the enthusiasm for the whole hour. In baseball, there is the "bases loaded, no outs" as well as "two out, nobody on." But for this show, it starts with "*Allez cuisine!*" and it's "extra innings, bases loaded, no outs" until the end. It's tough talking with that enthusiasm for the whole hour. I can't take a breather anywhere.

At the beginning, I was telling people that I couldn't very well keep saying, "The knife goes up! The knife is down!" But during the rehearsal, when I said, "Oh! A new ingredient" Mr. Hattori took over and talked away. That's when I thought that I may live through this experience. It was Mr. Hattori's unending talk that kept this program going.

I tasted a dish just once over the 6 years. I was a judge then, and it was really confusing being a broadcaster as well as a judge. In baseball it would be like being the pitcher and being the umpire as well. That was the first and last time that I tasted any of the dishes.

They said that those dishes were especially good, but I found it difficult to describe the taste.

I still don't know a single thing about cooking. Whatever I didn't understand, I asked Mr. Hattori during the show.

You have to come up with an opinion after one or two mouthfuls. After this experience I realized that judges had a tough job, too. I preferred being in the broadcasting seat.

TESTIMONY OF THE CAST AND STAFF

Hanako Asao

(Assistant Producer, Nihon Telework, K.K.)

Six years ago, when the show first started, the primary job of the guest chefs was to keep their restaurants running. The restaurants lose momentum when the chefs go on the *Iron Chef.*

Once it had been decided that they will be on the show, the chefs all tell me that they are unable to sleep and unable to concentrate on their jobs for at least a week before the taping. Most of them show up with red eyes, the result of an all-nighter.

Before the show started, I went to several chefs to seek their advice. Not one of them supported the idea of the show. They've forgotten all this now that the show has been a hit. But back then, it was unthinkable that Chinese, Japanese, and European cuisines would compete on the same battlefield. I went to many chefs, asking them to be on the show. Obviously, they'd never heard of the show

The chefs all told me they couldn't sleep for a week before the taping.

then; and even after an explanation, their only reaction was "What is that anyway?" The few chefs who agreed to be on the show were very courageous people.

It's interesting to see the difference in speed of those early matches. In the beginning, the whole battle had a much slower speed. Chefs took their time in making their dishes, so there were

only two or three dishes that were made in each session. But little by little, chefs started to become serious about winning. They came armed with battle plans and it became a standard to prepare four to five dishes.

The dishes created in Kitchen Stadium changed, as did the dishes offered in restaurants. Restaurants offering a menu based on a mix of Japanese, Chinese, and Western foods appeared. At the restaurant of a chef who won in Battle Chinese Cabbage, Chinese cabbages appeared as the main item. I am glad for the opportunity to have been in the midst of all these changes.

The many laughter and tears that I shed in negotiating with the chefs are all a part of a wonderful memory now.

Yukio Hattori's Prestige Menu

Fusion Course

In recent years, a new type of cuisine called fusion has been popular in New York. It is a mixture of the different characteristics of food worldwide. In the twenty-first century, I think this type of cooking, which is not bound to a certain label, will become the main basis of ethnic cooking. The theme for the dishes I have chosen for this course is "fusion," and these dishes incorporate the different types of cuisine.

Papaya China Sandwich (Battle 174: Papaya)

Fried papaya wrapped with yuba is used as the skin of Peking ducks are used, and sandwiched between toasted bread spread with sweet miso and leeks. The result is an eclectic mixture of Japanese, Chinese, and South Asian flavors.

Avocado-Flavored Baby Chicken with Truffles and Tomatoes (Battle 86: Avocado)

A cold puree of avocados is spread on the breast meat of a baby chicken. Tomatoes marinated in vinaigrette are used as bedding for the chicken. The avocados enhance the taste of the chicken and the acidic tomatoes blend together to create a well-balanced taste.

Spicy Tuna Jaw and Backbone (Battle 220: Tuna)

The jaw and backbone of the tuna are flavored with mixed spice and cooked over charcoal. The spiciness is reminiscent of Southeast Asian flavors. The kama and ribs are the tastiest parts of a tuna, but tend to be malodorous. The smell of the fish is deleted by the use of spice, and only the tastiness remains.

Ravioli of Squid Ink Soup and Palm-Sized Sushi (Battle 291: Squid)

The squid ink soup, flavored with celery and lemongrass, is very similar to Thailand's Tom Yum Kun. Squid ink is usually only used in pastas and risottos, so this soup is very unique.

Hotpot of Sea Bass (Battle 38: Sea Bass)

This joint effort by Mr. Michiba and Mr. Chen was created during the Tag Match. The traditional Japanese dish of hotpot is eaten with ponzu soy sauce and tobanjan (hot red chili paste). It's a delightful mix of a Japanese dish eaten with Chinese flavoring.

Sea Bream Cracker with Anzu Liquor Ice Cream
(Battle 221: Sea Bream)

After the many different flavors of an ethnic course, a light, refreshing dessert is called for. A thin slice of sea bream is deep fried and used as a kind of wafer to garnish the ice cream.

IRON CHEF

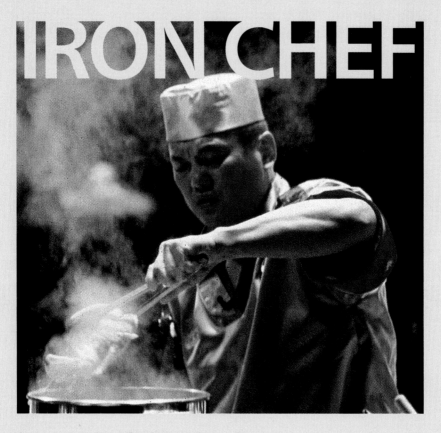

Masaharu Morimoto

(The Third Iron Chef Japanese)

I was already in New York when the *Iron Chef* started, but I knew of the program. There are several companies in New York that tape Japanese programs and rent them out to Japanese companies and restaurants. The show was in several of these videotapes. I was amazed at what they did when I watched these shows. These Iron Chefs seemed to be at ease in creating dishes in a mere hour, and their assistants seemed to know exactly what the Iron Chefs wanted. It looked like the Iron Chefs were at an advantage. When I actually became one, I found out it wasn't like that at all.

When they came to me with an offer to become an Iron Chef, I honestly thought that I wasn't up to the job. Perhaps once, as a challenger, but regularly seemed an impossible task. I started out as a sushi chef, and after going to New York, I mixed different cuisines in order to please the multicultural market there. My style was a mixture of all the good parts of different cuisines. I wasn't a specialist of any one type of cooking. I had never mastered traditional Japanese cooking, or French cooking, so I had no basics. I didn't think a person like myself was cut out to become an Iron Chef in Japanese cuisine.

> **It looks like the Iron Chefs are at an advantage. When I actually became one, I found out it is not like that at all.**

So why did I accept the offer? It all boils down to the fact that I like being in the center of attention and I am competitive. If I turned it down, someone else would have taken the job. I didn't want to regret my decision when I saw another person doing what I would have been doing. I accepted the position of Iron Chef, thinking that it was better to regret something after doing it, then regret not having done it at all.

After I actually did accept the position, I wasn't exactly scared, but I was really nervous. The first battle was the height of my nervousness. In the plane coming back from New York, I prayed that the plane would crash. I wished that it would crash and I would end up with a broken leg or something. Then there would be an article in a newspaper with a heading like, "Iron Chef injured in a plane crash from New York. Battle to be postponed." But I got back home safely, and I was crestfallen. I was that nervous.

I knew fully what was expected of me when I accepted the offer.

They chose me out of all the wonderful Japanese chefs in Japan because, having been in New York, they expected me to do something out of the ordinary. I strived to create a dish that was "unique, avant-garde, and yet delicious" for every episode. It's easier said than done. Since ancient times, certain ingredients have been said to go with certain ingredients. But if I followed these rules, the dish would end up being ordinary. It ends up being ordinary because it's a good combination and it tastes good. So what I did was deny the basic rules and combine things that would, in all probability, not go well together. I had to start from "couldn't possibly eat this" to something that would pass muster on the program. There aren't many dishes that are unique, avant-garde, yet delicious in this world.

I had to cook edible dishes out of inedible ingredients . . . thinking of recipes practically gave me ulcers.

I had made a resolution during my trip from New York. The dishes I had been making in New York were interesting and different. I decided that I would use those dishes one by one on the show. But during a simulation session at the Gourmet Academy, I made all those dishes and asked them what they thought. The reply was that all of these dishes had already been made on the show. I was in a panic. I had used up all of my secret recipes in the first battle. Caviar and miso spread on potato chips, oil on sashimi, or frying flattened sardines and using

them as garnishes . . . all of them were used in the first battle. During the match, all I thought about was winning, so I used all the ideas that I knew of, but afterward, I regretted it. What was I to do now?

Well, I made up new

recipes as I went along, but still in the last six months, I had to come up with something really original by myself. It was really hard. Thinking of new recipes practically gave me ulcers. It didn't help matters when Mr. Fukui, the broadcaster, said things like, "Let's see what Mr. Morimoto is going to do with this ingredient!" I did what a graduate of an elite university, supervising the development of a new product for a huge food corporation, does . . . and I did it for every show.

Your biggest enemy in Kitchen Stadium is not the opponent or the time. It is you, yourself. Winning or losing isn't the point (well, I was never happy about losing . . .). It's whether what you are aiming to create is created to your satisfaction and whether or not the judges can understand what you had created. It's when these two things don't happen that I am most disappointed.

> What we demand of an Iron Chef of Japanese cuisine is a dish that the whole world can appreciate. It has to be world cuisine.

During my introductory video clip, Mr. Kaga said, "What we demand of an Iron Chef of Japanese cuisine is a dish that the whole world can appreciate. It has to be world cuisine. I chose him regardless of many oppositions, because I believed that he could do just that." It took a while for the judges to truly understand what I was doing and why I was doing them. "What part of this dish is Japanese? It's good, but it isn't Japanese," was one of the first comments that I received. But the judges slowly started to understand what I was doing. The best example of that would be Masumi Okada.

Mr. Okada was present as a judge during my first battle (Battle Sea Bream). I had won the battle 3 to 1, and Mr. Okada was the only one who hadn't given me his vote. His reasoning was, "It was good, and it had panache. But this isn't a Japanese dish that an Iron Chef would make. I would rather give my vote to a taste that I am familiar with, then to something I don't understand." So at the next battle that Mr. Okada judged, which was Battle Tofu—and the one after that—Battle Baby Salmon—I focused entirely on Mr. Okada and cooked for him. Then his comment changed to, "This difference is interesting. It's good. I never tasted anything like this." He had rejected my cooking at first because of the "difference," but now the "difference" was good. I was supremely happy to see this change.

What I had been doing as an Iron Chef is being done everywhere now. It's called *creative cuisine.* The judges accepted my cooking because the distance between my cooking and the norm of society had started to lessen. It was the times that helped me. It was all good timing.

I fought twenty-four battles as an Iron Chef, but I never became relaxed. When they call out, *"Allez cuisine!"* and I grip my knife, I become relaxed, but up until that moment, I had my fears. When the theme ingredient is announced, it may turn out to be the thing you least expect. So until I held my knife, I was always tense. You hear about how people doing kendo relax once they are holding anything, even chopsticks. It's the same with us. Once we are holding our knives, we know where to begin. But until then, I'm shaking all over.

Overtimes always unnerved me. The match is finished, the judges taste them and declare a tie. We are herded out of the studio while they are bringing the new theme ingredient in. Once we are back inside, they announce the ingredient, and then it's *"Allez cuisine!"* all over again. For regular battles, we have time to look over the ingredients before the battle. But there is none of that for overtimes. Most of the ingredients have been used up in the previous match so you're not sure what is left. It would be much easier if we were given the time to see what ingredients were left. It's like, Leeks! None!

What I had been doing as an Iron Chef is being done everywhere now. It's called *creative cuisine.*

I had to panic, figuring out what to do about no leeks.

People comment, "Good thing you became famous" after I did my stint as an Iron Chef, but the notion still hasn't sunk in. Nothing has changed for me, and I don't know how this will affect me yet. I have accumulated a lot of stress over the past 5 years, even before becoming an Iron Chef. I have gained weight, and my liver has been acting up. What if I die 5 years later, amid all these congratulatory words? Then nothing has come out of my being an Iron Chef. The real battle for Masaharu Morimoto begins now. I plan on opening my own restaurant in New York in the year 2001. I plan to go as far as I can as a chef. Do I have a chance? Of course I do. Failing in Tokyo is one thing, but I cannot afford to fail in New York. I will succeed in New York.

The real battle for Masaharu Morimoto begins now. I plan to go as far as I can as a chef.

BATTLES 251 TO 297

Show No.	Japanese Air Date	Challenger	Iron Chef	Battle	Judges
251	10/16/98	Kyouko Kagata	Chen	Veal	Tenmei Kano, Kayoko Kishimoto, Korn, Asako Kishi
252	10/23/98	Tatsutoshi Kumamoto	Morimoto	Natto	Tenmei Kano, Hiromi Nagasaku, Tsurutaro Kataoka, Chieko Honma
253	10/30/98	Kensuke Sakai	Kobe	Pumpkin	Shinichiro Kurimoto, Kayoko Kishimoto, Shigeo Nagashima, Asako Kishi
254	11/6/98	Kazumi Nagayama	Sakai	Saury	Shinichiro Kurimoto, Kuniko Asagi, Joji Yamamoto, Kazuko Saiki
255	11/13/98	Hisao Yaginuma	Chen	Cilantro	Tenmei Kanou, Yukio Hatoyama, Sachi Hatoyama, Kazuko Saiki
256	11/20/98	Takatugu Sasaoka	Kobe	Wild Maitake Mushroom	Shinichiro Kurimoto, Yoko Akino, Panzetta Girolamo, Asako Kishi
257	11/27/98	Marco Morinari	Morimoto	Porcini Mushroom	Shinichiro Kurimoto, Chizuru Azuma, Francesco Espogito, Kazuko Saiki
258	12/4/98	Mitsuo Hazama	Sakai	Duck	Shinichiro Kurimoto, Keiko Saito, Masumi Okada, Asako Kishi

Show No.	Japanese Air Date	Challenger	Iron Chef	Battle	Judges
259	12/11/98	Hiromichi Yoneda	Kobe	Octopus	Tenmei Kanou, Naomi Hosokawa, Hideki Takahashi, Asako Kishi
260	12/18/98	Mitsuo Suganuma	Chen	Shark's Fin	Shinichiro Kurimoto, Yoko Akino, Chai Ran, Kazuko Saiki
261	12/25/98	Jiro Ogue	Morimoto	Turkey	Yasushi Akimoto, Miwako Fujitani, Kinya Kitaoji, Asako Kishi
262	1/8/99	Kaken Sya	Chen	Homard	Tenmei Kanou, Hisako Manda, Shukou Sasaki, Kazuko Saiki
263	1/15/99	Kouei Kamimura	Sakai	Codfish	Shinichiro Kurimoto, Yoko Akino, Tsurutaro Kataoka, Kazuko Saiki
264	1/22/99	Constantino Genmoli	Kobe	Green Pepper	Youichi Masuzoe, Megumi Ooishi, Tenmei Kanou, Asako Kishi
265	1/29/99	Hiroyuki Hakogi	Morimoto	Yellowtail	Shinichiro Kurimoto, Keiko Saito, Mitsuo Tatsukawa, Kazuko Saiki
266	2/5/99	Tetsuji Iio	Morimoto	Taraba Crab	Tenmei Kanou, Hiromi Nagasaku, Katuya Nomura, Kazuko Saiki
267	2/12/99	Hironobu Tujiguchi	Kobe	Chocolate Banana	Shinichiro Kurimoto, Akiko Hinagata, Tetsuya Kumagawa, Asako Kishi

Show No.	Japanese Air Date	Challenger	Iron Chef	Battle	Judges
268	2/19/99	Toshiya Senba	Sakai	Asyura Oyster	Tenmei Kanou, Lisa Jyunna, Masahiko Kondo, Asako Kishi
269	2/26/99	Ryouzo Asao	Chen	Shark	Shinichiro Kurimoto, Michie Nakamaru, Masumi Okada, Asako Kishi
270	3/12/99	Koumei Nakamura	Morimoto	Egg	Shinichiro Kurimoto, Yuko Asano, Kotaro Satomi, Kazuko Saiki
271	3/19/99	Kouji Hosokai	Sakai	Oxtail	Shinichiro Kurimoto, Keiko Saito, Korn, Kazuko Saiki
272	3/26/99	Seiya Masahara	Morimoto	Angler	Tenmei Kanou, Keiko Masuda, Hideki Takahashi, Kazuko Saiki
273	4/2/99	Gyokubun Sai	Chen	Chinese Cabbage	Shinichiro Kurimoto, Kayoko Kishimoto, Shinji Tanimura, Asako Kishi
274	4/9/99	Tooru Komori	Sakai	Udon Noodle	Tenmei Kanou, Miwako Fujitani, Toru Watanabe, Asako Kishi
275	4/16/99	Franco Canzoniere	Kobe	Tomato	Shinichiro Kurimoto, Chizuru Azuma, Panzetta Girolamo, Kazuko Saiki
276	4/23/99	Yusuke Yamashita	Morimoto	Codfish Roe	Shinichiro Kurimoto, Sachiko Kobayashi, Kunihiko Mitamura, Kazuko Saiki

Show No.	Japanese Air Date	Challenger	Iron Chef	Battle	Judges
277	4/30/99	Yusuke Yamashita	Morimoto	Long Leek	Shinichiro Kurimoto, Sachiko Kobayashi, Kunihiko Mitamura, Kazuko Saiki
278	5/7/99	Takeshi Ookubo	Chen	Bean Sprout	Shinichiro Kurimoto, Akiko Hinagata, Takao Horiuchi, Yoshiko Ishii
279	5/14/99	Michel Usel	Sakai	Lamb	Tenmei Kanou, Akiko Nishina, Kazuyoshi Nagashima, Asako Kishi
280	5/21/99	Spano Stelvio	Chen	Milk-Fed Pork	Shinichiro Kurimoto, Chizuru Azuma, Hideki Takahashi, Asako Kishi
281	6/11/99	Makoto Nagata	Kobe	Jumbo Lobster	Tenmei Kanou, Naomi Hosokawa, Tsurutaro Kataoka, Kazuko Saiki
282	6/18/99	Keiji Nakazawa	Morimoto	Shad, Conglers, Tuna, Egg, Kanpyo	Shinichiro Kurimoto, Miyoko Asada, Asei Kobayashi, Asako Kishi
283	6/25/99	Tsutomu Makio	Sakai	Black Pork	Shinichiro Kurimoto, Yoko Akino, Toshio Shiba, Kazuko Saiki
284	7/2/99	Michael Noble	Morimoto	Potato	Tenmei Kanou, Yoko Akino, Yukio Hahsi, Asako Kishi
285	7/9/99	Yuji Tateno	Chen	Sea Urchin	Keiko Saito, Ishihara, Tim Zagat, Nina Zagat

Show No.	Japanese Air Date	Challenger	Iron Chef	Battle	Judges
286	7/16/99	Yoshimi Tanigkawa	Morimoto	Sea Eel	Tenmei Kanou, Yukiyo Toake, Tsurutaro Kataoka, Yoshiko Ishii
287	7/23/99	Shouji Yamaoka	Kobe	Jumbo Mushroom	Tenmei Kanou, Sae Isshiki, Kazuhiko Kato, Asako Kishi
288	7/30/99	Dominic Corby	Chen	Foie Gras	Tenmei Kanou, Yuko Asano, Isao Fukutome, Kazuko Saiki
289	8/6/99	Dominic Corby	Chen	Asparagus	Tenmei Kanou, Yuko Asano, Isao Fukutome, Kazuko Saiki
290	8/13/99	Hiromoto Sakai	Kobe	Conger	Shinichiro Kurimoto, Kayoko Kishimoto, Kiyoshi Nakajyo, Kazuko Saiki
291	8/20/99	Akira Watanabe	Morimoto	Squid	Shinichiro Kurimoto, Megumi Oosihi, Ryuko Hagiwara, Kazuko Saiki
292	8/27/99	Yoshihide Furuga	Sakai	Ray	Tenmei Kanou, Hisako Manda, Kinya Kitaoji, Kazuko Saiki
293	9/3/99	Ryozo Shigematsu	Morimoto	Sea Bass	Shinichiro Kurimoto, Yumi Takigawa, Hideki Takahashi, Asako Kishi
294	9/10/99	Kobe	Chen	Tokyo X (Strongest Iron Chef Battle)	Tenmei Kanou, Momoko Kikuchi, Akebono, Asako Kishi, Hiroshi Ishinabe

Show No.	Japanese Air Date	Challenger	Iron Chef	Battle	Judges
295	9/19/99	Morimoto	Sakai	Green Pepper (Strongest Iron Chef Battle)	Shinichiro Kurimoto, Kyoko Shinno, Kinya Kitaoji, Kazuko Saiki, Rokusaburo Michiba
296	9/24/99	Kenichi Chen	Sakai	Homard (Strongest Iron Chef Battle)	Tatsuo Umemiya, Yuko Asano, Kyoko Mano, Kazuko Saiki, Rokusaburo Michiba
297	9/24/99	Alain Passart	Sakai	Ronkonkai Chicken (Strongest Iron Chef Battle)	Ryutaro Hashimoto, Yoshiko Mita, Tatsuo Umemiya, Chai Ran, Asako Kishi

TESTIMONY OF THE CAST AND STAFF

Shinichiro Ota

(Narrator, Seiji Production)

When I first heard of the job, I was meant to be doing only the pilot episode. Because I wasn't scheduled to appear on screen, there were no outfits for me, and I was dressed in jeans. I wore whatever I wore when I came to the studio in the morning.

I was never on screen and I don't remember talking much either, in the beginning. I wonder when I started appearing on screen? Originally, Mr. [Masahiro] Ito, the scriptwriter, was supposed to be doing the talking as well.

> **I battled constantly with trying to convey a feeling of immediacy.**

When I watch the videos of the first few shows, I find that I am talking very slowly. I talked faster and faster as time went on. After the show got a different time slot, they wanted more of an "auto racing pit report" feel to the whole thing.

In my business as a narrator, mistakes are not allowed. But for this program, they allowed a few mistakes because it contributed to the feeling of immediacy. I made more than a few mistakes, so many in fact, that I got yelled at by the editing staff.

Though it is a variety show, there is nothing fake about it, so it is important to speak at the right time. If I don't say, "The chef used the wrong ingredient now" at that moment, the comment dies. That's timing. Even if I said it later, all the editing in the world would not be able to convey the immediacy. Oftentimes Mr. Ito yelled at me to use the comments "now." Sometimes I yelled back that I didn't have the time to use it "now." It's fine when you're able to use scripted comments at the right time, but when you lose the timing, and you are struggling to use it elsewhere, that is when it's most stressful.

I misread many of the characters. I said "sparrow's nest" instead of "swallow's nest," or instead of reading it as "*bei nasu*" I misread it as "*kome nasu*." It was a given that those ingredients be misread. Well, it shouldn't be, but it happened. I also misread several of the challengers' names. Mr. Ito's handwriting is illegible. He throws the words down on paper and hands it to me. But I got used to his handwriting. All writers have their own messy handwriting. After a while I got so good, that I was able to decipher words that even he himself couldn't.

I would like to meet the man doing my voiceover in America. I hear he is fat like me.

It only happened once, but there was a time when an Iron Chef scolded me. Mr. Tanaka, the director, told me to go and interview the Iron Chef during the battle. I thought it was a bad idea, but I figured, Why not, and stuck a microphone out to Mr. Chen Kenichi. He yelled, "Not now!" I totally understood that it was a bad time to conduct an interview, but I was hurt nonetheless. Mr. Tanaka understood, too, and we never interviewed chefs during a battle again.

I heard that this show is popular in the States now, and that they air it two times a week. My voice, along with Mr. Fukui and Mr. Hattori, is a voiceover. I have done voiceovers, but

have never had one done to me. My voice is high-pitched, and my words tend to get stuck in my throat. Instead of saying, "Fukui-san," it comes out as "kkui-san." I heard that the person doing the voiceover will get his words stuck at the same parts. High level indeed. I would like to meet him once. I hear he is fat like me. There are many top-level narrators in my office, but I think that I am the only one who got his voice dubbed. I'm the only one who has debuted internationally.

I was a 22-year-old novice who didn't know right from left when they told me to go do this job. I never thought that it would last this long. It's the longest I have ever stayed at one single job.

When I heard that the show was ending, I was sad, but on the other hand, relieved that I was able to do it until the very end. I am glad to have been able to be the "refrigerator reporter" until the very end.

Because this show was such an influential show, many people think that I am an announcer. Or I get jobs requesting that I use the *Iron Chef* style. I am not an announcer at Fuji Television. Please direct all inquiries to Aoji Productions.

I am glad that a novice like me was able to stay on as the "refrigerator reporter" until the very end.

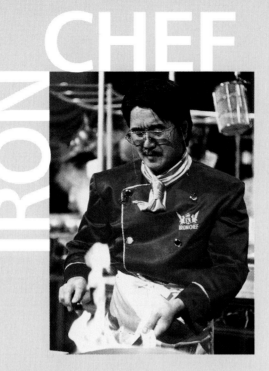

IRON CHEF

Hiroyuki Sakai

(The Second Iron Chef French)

Mr. Kihachi Kumagai, the owner of the Kihachi Restaurant, recommended me when he learned that the show was looking for a new Iron Chef of French cuisine. Every night, Mr. Matsuo and his staff would come to my restaurant to talk to me about it.

At the end, I met with the producers at Mr. Kumagai's restaurant. They convinced me to be on the show, saying that they only planned to be on the air for another 6 months, which meant battling maybe 2 or 3 times. The staff at the restaurant convinced me too, saying, "Monsieur, if it's only 3 times, why not?" I decided to take them up on their offer.

But it ended up being a 6-year stint. . . .

At first many people had much to say to me. "That program is a disgrace to the professionals"; "I can't believe he'd take over for Mr. Ishinabe; they are friends, for God's sake"; and so on.

But I was determined, having accepted it, to do whatever I had to do, regardless of what people might think.

It would be a lie to say that these words didn't matter to me. Negative comments like, "He is bringing French chefs down by being on such a low-level show"; "Cooking in a battle is ridiculous"; "How do they expect a decent French dish in a mere hour?" and so on were hurled at me all the time.

I kept telling my staff and those close to me that now that I was a part of the show, I would never do anything that might trouble the people on the show. I will do what I have said that I will do. I think those around me understood me.

> I was only meant to be on the show three times; I ended up staying for 6 years.

It was encouraging to have Mr. Michiba and Mr. Chen be so supportive of me in this situation.

The Iron Chefs have a special bond because we know that no one can fully comprehend the struggles that we go through except for ourselves. Obviously, there were differences in our genre and age, but our bond was very strong. Mr. Michiba, Mr. Chen, and I are 12 years apart from each other. Mr. Michiba was the father figure, while Mr. Chen saw me as an older brother. We supported each other psychologically as well.

We all owned our own restaurants, so we shared the problems we faced in our restaurants. We were truly very close.

After about a year or so, the ratings started to go up. The perspec-

The Iron Chefs have a special bond; we know no one else can fully comprehend the struggles we go through.

tive people had on the show started to change, bit by bit. People started taking on an attitude of, "Wow, it's a wonder how you keep up with it." At the beginning, no one believed that we really taped everything in one hour. "You have more than an hour, right?" they'd say. But after a while, they started to believe that, yes, we only had an hour, really.

They were amazed and impressed by the fact that we were only told of the theme ingredients then and by the fact that we could prepare such a meal in a mere hour.

The first time I lost, Mr. Matsuo said to me, "Mr. Sakai, aren't you a bit relieved now?" In truth, I was mortified. I think I lost in my ninth battle, a battle using homards.

It was worse that the opponent was a young French chef who had his own restaurant. I was scared to go back to my restaurant. My family's faces, my daughter's face came to mind . . . my daughter's friends had started to know what I did for a living, because they saw me on TV.

I was apprehensive about what my staff would say to me. I didn't want to go straight back to the restaurant. In the end, I was ultra-cheerful and I went in saying, "Hey, I lost today!" But everyone in the restaurant looked totally miserable. That was tough.

I wondered how my family would react. When I had first decided to become an Iron Chef, my family, especially my wife, was dead set against the idea. She was opposed to it for a long time. In the end she came around and became my biggest supporter. She told me she was glad that I had done it.

I was mortified when I lost for the first time.

My daughter was 14, 15 years old at the time. She would get teased by her friends at school, "Your dad lost yesterday, huh?"

My son was already working, and when people at his office found out what I did, his boss said to him, "So you're an Iron Chef's son." Many people from his office started coming to my restaurant, for which I am very grateful.

Many have asked me whether my son was going to follow in my footsteps. He seems to have absolutely no interest in food, so he probably can't take over as a chef. Maybe, in the future, he can join the company as a manager. But only if he so wishes.

Looking back, I never lost a battle

involving fish. I love fish. Everything is fine when I have confidence, but once I lose it, I made it a point to taste the opponent's dishes. When I still had doubts, I listened to the judges' comments regarding the opponent's dishes. I looked at how much of the food had been left behind by the judges. I believed that that would teach me a lesson as well.

I think it's important to observe the work of other chefs. When the opponent flavored a dish in a different way, I would grab one of his assistants and ask what it was flavored with.

Just once, I wanted to create the perfect dish. When my favorite ingredient was announced one day, I decided that I would only cook one dish. It would be the perfect dish. My assistants can sit and watch, and I would do everything by myself. I wanted to show them that the best you can do is cook one perfect dish in an hour. But I couldn't. My dream for a perfect dish was never realized.

I hated Battle Octopus. When I learned that it was a battle of octopusi, I lost all interest. I don't like mollusks.

I am grateful to the show for giving me the opportunity to deal with many types of ingredients, ingredients that I don't ordinarily use in French cooking. Asked what changed about me after becoming an Iron Chef, I would have to say nothing, since I am still the same. But one thing for sure is that I learned a lot.

Among the many challengers, there are ones who are weighed under the pressure of a big hotel. They carry with them all of the hotel's expectations. I tend to be more careful toward them, regardless of whether they win or lose. "It's only a TV show, don't be too uptight about it," is how I greet them.

I always pay attention to fan letters as well. I don't mind writing, so I write back to all the fan letters that I receive. I don't want these people, who have taken the time to write to me after watching the show, to wonder if their letters ever got to the Iron Chefs. All it takes is one postcard to show my appreciation. In some of those fan letters it is written that that person wrote because they heard that I always write back.

For the final battle between Mr. Chen and myself, there was a week between the preliminary battle and the final battle. Usually we talk to each other during the week, but for that particular week, neither of us called the other. When leaving the studio after the preliminary battle, we parted with the words, "Let's each of us do our best."

When the day finally came, and the theme was homards, I thought

that I would surely lose. It was pure luck that I won that day. After the battle, Mr. Chen and I embraced each other, and we were both so moved, we became teary. We were both tense. I wondered if my glasses would crack.

Chen and I were comrades, and we had a certain understanding. A year of so after Mr. Michiba left the show, Mr. Chen was talking of quitting. We had an unspoken pact even before then, that if either one of us leaves the show, the other would follow. Well, Mr. Chen's mother had just died, and that led him to consider quitting.

But after talking to Mr. Michiba and Mr. Matsuo, I said to him that since we came this far, we might as well go through with it until the very end. We decided to concentrate on enjoying ourselves.

When the *Iron Chef* ended, I was sad. From now on, Friday nights will never be the same.

I was glad for the opportunity to show my way of life for the past 6 years. I think that a kind of "proof" of myself as a chef was made through this show, and I matured a lot as well. I am filled with gratefulness.

It was good for the culinary world that the laymen got a glimpse of what chefs are like. I felt, however, that there was an abundance of ingredients every time, and much of it was wasted. The whole lot wasn't on screen. I brought home all of the leftover ingredients.

TESTIMONY OF THE CAST AND STAFF

Yukio Hattori
(Principal of Hattori School of Nutrition)

I became involved with the show following an invitation from Mr. Matsuo, the producer. Not only was I involved as a commentator, I also attended the weekly meetings for the show. I helped decide the theme ingredients, and how to present them on the show.

The show's influence was amazing. I heard from an employee of a gourmet shop that after a particular episode, customers flocked there demanding foie gras. They wanted fresh foie gras in particular. The asso-

ciation of French ingredients was also surprised by this phenomenon. They had never seen anything like this. Aside from theme ingredients, other items grew in popularity. Balsamic vinegar in particular. They weren't widely known, even in the Japanese culinary world, before this time. But after the chefs used them on the show, consumption grew 350 percent annually.

Of course, none of this happened overnight. When the show first aired, many chefs attacked me, saying, "Cancel the show! It'll bring down the whole culinary world!" After a while, such opposition petered out.

Even a few of the judges asked, "Are these people doing it for real?"

I am sure that everyone was surprised. There never had been anything like *Iron Chef* before. Even a few of the judges asked, "Are these people doing it for real?"

If everyone hadn't been so serious about it, it wouldn't have lasted for 6 years. It caught the attention of the viewers because they could feel the seriousness between the Iron Chefs and the challengers. A pinch of salt alone can make or break a dish.

It was the same for the staff members. While many similar programs have been canceled, this one grew in popularity to a point where they air it twice a week in the United States. I heard that the Americans were amazed with this show. They couldn't believe we had such a sophisticated culture in Japan, the land of Fujiyama and geishas.

None of this was coincidence. Details were important to us. For example, for table settings, if it was Japanese food, the correct setting for Japanese cuisine was used. The same is true for Western food. We didn't want anyone to see it and point out that it was culturally incorrect or anything like that. Correct wineglasses were paired with certain wines; and for Japanese cuisine, the seasonality was strictly adhered to. Perhaps this is only the basics, but it is true that many of these rules have been done away with in recent years. We always did our research. Such attention to details resulted in *Iron Chef* being an authentic show.

As far as I know, no other show has ever influenced the culinary world as this show has. The culinary world is a very traditional world. Chefs dare not break out of the mold. Many do not welcome the influence of this show, but it has changed the culinary world in at least two ways.

The first influence is that the *Iron Chef* has proven that new dishes, transcending a particular genre, can be created. The other influence is the realization that using as many ingredients as one wishes can create dishes. This is a novel experience for chefs. Cost is a major issue for them. For Mr. Michiba's "Dashi of Life," he used a potful of the most expensive bonito flakes, which are about 660 yen (about $6.00) per ounce. Even at the most expensive restaurants, such extravagance would not be tolerated. I used to request that the challengers create "not everyday dishes, but dishes worthy of the Paris collection!" It is my wish that every chef experience this at least once in his or her career. Even through a surreal experience as TV, there was some positive effect on the challengers who did experience it.

I heard Americans were amazed with this show. They couldn't believe we had such a sophisticated culture in Japan.

The biggest products of this show are the superstar chefs. Until then, chefs had been backstage; now they are stars in their own right. Even the sweat on their brows looks smart, and I'm sure that everyone was shocked to realize that chefs too can afford Mercedes. Chefs were not hip until now.

This new view is reflected in the questionnaires of elementary school children. When the *Iron Chef* first started, the profession of chef ranked 18th in their dream professions. After a while, it went up to the 3rd best profession, and last year, it ranked as the number one dream profession. While I don't know how many of these children will end up becoming chefs, I do believe many more will attempt to become one. Though only the gifted few can become chefs, with a larger selection of these gifted few, the skill of chefs is sure to increase.

The *Iron Chef* has undoubtedly made its mark on the culinary world.

As I have mentioned before, many of the basic traditions have been done away with recently. On the other hand, as contradictory as it may sound, there was a wall of tradition that blocked any new progress. It won't happen overnight, but I hope that the new generation of chefs who have grown up watching this show will breathe new air into the culinary world.

Sustained by this wish, I was able to go on for 6 years. If everyone had been halfhearted in their involvement, these influences would not have been made. Because of our determinations, many chefs who had opposed this show came to accept it. Individuals who had rejected any mention of the *Iron Chef* seemed to be sorry to hear that the show was ending. I was filled with such emotion during the last taping, as I am sure all of the staff was. Memories of the 6 years ran through my mind like a movie. No words could begin to describe my feelings then.

TESTIMONY OF THE CAST AND STAFF

Asako Kishi
(Culinary Journalist)

There was a good representation of every age group in the judges on the show. Mr. Masaaki Hirano and I were in our 60s and 70s. Mr. Shinichiro Kurimoto, the late Mr. Tamio Kageyama, and Mr. Tenmei Kanou were in their 40s and 50s. And there were young actors and actresses who were in their 20s. Some of them were as young as 18. So there was a wide variety of age and gender.

All the judges had sure tongues, and they were knowledgeable

about foods. However, in order to avoid having the loser be totally put down by the judges, there was nobody extreme. The guests were a different story, but the regular judges were chosen with such criteria in mind.

Whenever I give a lecture somewhere, many question me on whether the food was actually good or whether the chefs cooked in an hour. Some dishes were very good, but there were cases where the potential of a particular ingredient had been ruined. Plus the time constraint didn't help matters. For example, there were several cases where I felt that the dish would have been tastier if it had been cooked a little longer.

Another example that I always give is Battle Truffle. Professor Hattori was preparing a dish where thinly sliced pieces of truffle were placed on top of a sea bass pie. The crust of the pie was supposed to have been flaky, but due to lack of time, it turned out all mushy.

I never had the heart to tell a chef that his dish wasn't good.

But I never had the heart to tell a chef that his dish wasn't good, especially after seeing them sweat and toil for the past hour. So, I always tried to avoid the word *good* whenever commenting on the dish. Instead I would say things like, "The aroma is wonderful," "It goes down really well," "I love the crunchiness," and "You have really outdone yourself today."

When I first joined the *Shufu no Tomosya* as a journalist back in 1955, the first thing that I was taught was, "Try to convey how good a dish is without using the word *good*." This lesson has served me well. The color and shape can be conveyed through television and magazines, but taste and smell cannot be conveyed. It was tough, but it was a worthwhile experience.

When Mr. Sakai and Mr. Pierre Ganiere battled at the château in Angers, France, I likened Mr. Ganiere's cooking to "a dagger, posed and

ready to strike, inching closer and closer." The interpreter wouldn't inter-
pret these words, saying that such words do not exist in the French lan-
guage. I really felt then that describing dishes is difficult.

Cooking is a reflection of the chef's personality. The warmth, the
graciousness, all those characteristics come out in the dishes. For example, Mr. Michiba is a very gallant man. He is chivalrous in his cooking as
well. So his dishes end up having graciousness to them. Mr. Ishinabe's
dishes all seem to be singing French chansons. It's as if they were hum-
ming along while being made.

Mr. Chen, I've known him forever. I edited his
very first book, *Chen Kenichi's Chinese Menu.* A professor of the Women's College of Nutrition said to
me, "Kenichi needed the show *Iron Chef* in order to
outdo his father." Chen himself seems to agree, as he
has been heard saying pretty much the same thing
elsewhere.

> **Kenichi needed the show *Iron Chef* in order to outdo his father.**

Maybe it's because Mr. Sakai started out his career as a Japanese
chef, his dishes are beautiful in their presentation. He is much more sen-
sitive than he appears.

Mr. Koumei Nakamura. His knife skills are sublime, he creates
wonderful-tasting dishes, his
boiled vegetables are exceptional . . . I suppose this is
what Nadaman is all about.

Mr. Morimoto has a
good eye. And he hates to lose.
He is good at adapting to the
circumstances.

Mr. Kobe is someone

who can get his job done, while revolutionizing the industry. He is only 30, he has a great many years in his career left.

To all the chefs, "Everything tasted wonderful" and "Thank you for everything."

My motto is to "Eat well, eat healthy, live well, and die happy." I believe that eating good food is the key to happiness and preparing good food is the key to making others happy. Food is nutrition not only for the body but also for the soul. I would like to eat well and lead a happy life.

ANALYSIS OF THE SEVEN IRON CHEFS

The data of all 297 battles battled by the seven Iron Chefs have been compiled, and used in the analysis of the seven Iron Chefs. Data of their total score, winning rate, theme ingredients, and opposing chefs from different fields are all used to illustrate the complete picture of all their battles.

The calculation method is as follows:

For every match, 3 points are given to the winner, 0 to the loser, and 1 point each if it is a tie. In special matches (big battles), the winning points are doubled. Returning challengers, or "Revengers," are fierce opponents, and the winning points are doubled. Because Iron Chefs are the toughest opponents, matches against them give the winner quadrupled points. Should a match against a Revenger end in a tie, the points would be given as follows: 1 point for a tie times the winning point doubled equals 2 points. Should there be a victory against a fellow Iron Chef in a special match, the points would be as follows: 3 winning points times the winning point doubled for a special match times quadruple points given for winning against another Iron Chef equals 24 points. The sum of the winning points, divided by the number of battles is the Big Game (BG) deviation value. This number is used to measure how strong an Iron Chef is. The mean value of BG is 3; the higher you are above 3, the stronger you are.

The First French Iron Chef: Yutaka Ishinabe

Overall Results

Type of Battle	Win/Lose/Tie	Winning Rate (percent)
Overall (8 battles)	7/1/0	88
Tag Match	1/0/0	100
Versus a Revenger	1/0/0	100
Versus an Iron Chef	1/0/0	100
Special Battle (1 battle)	1/0/0	100

- **Longest winning streak: 4 battles**

- **Total points: 42**

- **BG deviation value: 5.25**

Results for Different Theme Ingredients

Ingredient	Win/Lose/Tie	Points	BG Deviation Value
Seafood	2/0/0	6	3.00
Vegetable	3/0/0	9	3.00
Meat	0/1/0	0	0
Other	2/0/0	27	13.50

Results against the Challengers

Cuisine	Win/Lose/Tie	Points	BG Deviation Value
French	3/1/0	9	2.25
Japanese	1/0/0	3	3.00
Italian	1/0/0	3	3.00
Chinese	2/0/0	27	13.50

Ishinabe marked his debut in the very first battle on *Iron Chef*. He took part in five battles that year, two battles in 1995, and one Special Battle in 1998. The only battle he lost was against Jacques Borie in Battle Chicken.

No deep analysis can be made of Ishinabe, due to the few number of battles. He has not battled against chefs of multicultural and ethnic cuisines, nor has he taken part in any overseas battles like Sakai and Chen. But he has managed to illustrate his true value in the 1998 Special Battle: The Host's 2000 Plate Battle. He took part in a Tag Match, teaming with Sakai and the notorious challenger Etsuo Jou against the fearsome trio of Chinese cuisine: Chen, Wakiya, and Miyamoto. He won the Special Battle and a Tag Match and won against an Iron Chef, grand slamming the point total. He is now a legendary figure in the culinary world.

The First Japanese Iron Chef: Rokusaburo Michiba

Overall Results

Type of Battle	Win/Lose/Tie	Winning Rate (percent)
Overall (38 battles)	32/5/1	84
Tag Match	1/1/0	50
Versus a Revenger	2/1/0	67
Versus an Iron Chef	1/1/0	50
Special Battle (6 battles)	5/1/0	83

- **Longest winning streak: 11 battles**

- **Total points: 139**

- **BG deviation value: 3.66**

Results for Different Theme Ingredients

Ingredient	Win/Lose/Tie	Points	BG Deviation Value
Seafood	16/2/0	63	3.50
Vegetable	7/1/1	25	2.78
Meat	4/1/0	36	7.20
Other	5/1/0	15	2.50

Results against the Challengers

Cuisine	Win/Lose/Tie	Points	BG Deviation Value
French	6/2/0	18	2.25
Japanese	10/1/0	39	3.55
Italian	3/0/0	12	4.00
Chinese	8/2/0	55	5.00
Multicultural	5/0/0	15	3.00

Michiba's winning rates are spectacular. He has won 84 percent of his battles; and with the exception of Ishinabe, he has the highest score. The number of battles compared to the other Iron Chefs isn't high, but he has used a wide variety of ingredients and won against chefs in a variety of cuisines.

His BG deviation value is higher than the average BG deviation value of 3, which means that he was strong in big battles as well. He was especially strong in meats, scoring a whopping 7.20. Winning the 1995 Iron Chef World Cup and winning the Mr. Iron Chef Battle are reflected in this score. He has won 83 percent of his Special Battles.

The only disappointing factor is his weak deviation value against French chefs. He lost his first two French battles, but he recovered well from those losses and won three consecutive times against French chefs after that. Michiba was an indomitable Iron Chef.

The Chinese Iron Chef: Chen Kenichi

Overall Results

Type of Battle	Win/Lose/Tie	Winning Rate (percent)
Overall (92 battles)	67/22/3	73
Tag Match	0/3/0	0
Versus a Revenger	1/3/1	27
Versus an Iron Chef	2/4/0	33
Special Battles (8 battles)	4/4/0	50

- **Longest winning streak: 14 battles**

- **Total points: 256**

- **BG deviation value: 2.78**

Results for Different Theme Ingredients

Ingredient	Win/Lose/Tie	Points	BG Deviation Value
Seafood	32/10/0	100	2.38
Vegetable	19/7/0	57	2.19
Meat	6/2/3	48	4.36
Other	10/3/0	51	3.92

Results against the Challengers

Cuisine	Win/Lose/Tie	Points	BG Deviation Value
French	5/5/2	42	3.50
Japanese	17/3/0	51	2.55
Italian	13/2/0	60	4.00
Chinese	25/10/1	82	2.28
Multicultural	7/2/0	21	2.33

Though Chen stayed with the *Iron Chef* for the whole 6 years, he was not blessed with many big victories. He never won a single Tag Match, and he often lost against Revengers and other Iron Chefs. At 22 losses, he had the most defeats of any Iron Chef.

But his battles were rich in content. Many viewers were touched when seeing him battle. He is the only chef to have taken part in eight Special Battles. With six contests, he has the highest number of battles against other Iron Chefs. He is the only Iron Chef to have battled against Ishinabe. Most important is his 9-month-long winning streak of 14 battles. Neither Michiba nor Sakai was able to accomplish such a feat. This record number of victories is a big part of the history of the *Iron Chef.*

Chen's biggest accomplishment, however, is his record of being on the show longest and taking part in the highest number of battles. His physical and mental strength is to be revered. He is probably the most memorable of all the Iron Chefs.

The Second French Iron Chef: Hiroyuki Sakai

Overall Results

Type of Battle	Win/Lose/Tie	Winning Rate (percent)
Overall (86 battles)	70/15/1	81
Tag Match	3/0/0	100
Versus a Revenger	5/2/0	71
Versus an Iron Chef	4/1/0	80
Special Battles (6 battles)	4/2/0	67

- **Longest winning streak: 9 battles (twice)**

- **Total points: 301**

- **BG deviation value: 3.50**

Results for Different Theme Ingredients

Ingredient	Win/Lose/Tie	Points	BG Deviation Value
Seafood	28/4/1	106	3.21
Vegetable	14/3/0	66	3.88
Meat	12/6/0	48	2.67
Other	16/2/0	81	4.50

Results against the Challengers

Cuisine	Win/Lose/Tie	Points	BG Deviation Value
French	31/8/1	106	2.65
Japanese	19/4/0	81	3.52
Italian	7/0/0	24	3.43
Chinese	8/2/0	66	6.60
Multicultural	5/1/0	24	4.00

It is obvious by looking at the data that Sakai was an Iron Chef with stellar statistics. At 81 percent, his winning rate rivals that of Michiba's. His winning point of 301 total points is the number one of all the Iron Chefs. He accumulated 60 of these points by winning the Last Holy War Special Battle series. He has had two consecutive winning streaks of 9 battles each. It was characteristic of him to win, without a ruffle, against an Italian challenger.

Careless mistakes are not a part of Sakai's dictionary, and he was indomitable in the big games as well. Undefeated at the Tag Matches, he won most of the Six Special Battles against Revengers and other Iron Chefs. The one time he lost against an Iron Chef was during the 1995 Mr. Iron Chef Battle against Chen.

Unfortunately, in matches against fellow French chefs, he lost eight times; and whenever the theme is meat, he does not do well. When he battled against a French chef with meat as the theme ingredient, he lost four times.

The Second Japanese Iron Chef: Koumei Nakamura

Overall Results

Type of Battle	Win/Lose/Tie	Winning Rate (percent)
Overall (37 battles)	24/11/1	67
Tag Match	0/1/0	0
Versus a Revenger	3/1/1	60
Versus an Iron Chef	2/1/0	67
Special Battles (3 battles)	2/1/0	50

- **Longest winning streak: 7 battles**

- **Total points: 118**

- **BG Deviation Value: 3.28**

Results for Different Theme Ingredients

Ingredient	Win/Lose/Tie	Points	BG Deviation Value
Seafood	12/5/0	45	2.65
Vegetable	1/0/0	3	3.00
Meat	5/2/1	22	2.75
Other	6/4/0	48	4.80

Results against the Challengers

Cuisine	Win/Lose/Tie	Points	BG Deviation Value
French	4/6/1	16	1.45
Japanese	12/3/0	72	4.80
Italian	0/1/0	0	0.00
Chinese	4/0/0	15	3.75
Multicultural	4/1/0	15	3.00

The data for Nakamura are very distinctive. Though his winning rate is not particularly high, his BG deviation value is over 3. This illustrates that he was strong when it came to the big battles.

He never did win in the Tag Matches, but he won a majority of the battles against the Revengers, other Iron Chefs, and the four Special Battles. The battles against the other Iron Chefs were won against the Iron Chefs of Japanese cuisine, Morimoto and Michiba. This resulted in a staggering BG deviation value for Japanese cuisine of 4.80. Though he lost the majority of battles against French chefs, it should be taken into account that this includes Battle Duck against Leprince and the Battle

Foie Gras against Passart (tie). Seeing that the deviation value for the theme ingredients are not bad, it could be said that Nakamura is a well-rounded chef. As for the battles against Chinese cuisine, he won all four of them. It's a pity he wasn't blessed with more opportunities to use vegetables, his strongest theme.

The Italian Iron Chef: Katsuhiko Kobe

Overall Results

Type of Battle	Win/Lose/Tie	Winning Rate (percent)
Overall (23 battles)	15/7/1	65
Tag Match	1/0/0	100
Versus a Revenger	0/2/0	0
Versus an Iron Chef	1/1/0	50
Special Battles (1 battle)	0/1/0	0

- **Longest winning streak: 5 battles (includes 1 tie)**

- **Total points: 55**

- **BG deviation value: 2.39**

Results for Different Theme Ingredients

Ingredient	Win/Lose/Tie	Points	BG Deviation Value
Seafood	4/2/1	13	1.86
Vegetable	7/1/0	21	2.63
Meat	0/1/0	0	0.00
Other	4/3/0	21	3.00

Results against the Challengers

Cuisine	Win/Lose/Tie	Points	BG Deviation Value
French	1/1/0	3	1.50
Japanese	1/2/1	4	1.00
Italian	7/1/0	21	2.63
Chinese	2/1/0	6	2.00
Multicultural	4/2/0	21	3.50

Kobe is the only Iron Chef without a winning debut battle. However, it must be remembered that his first battle was against a Revenger, Masahiko Hagiwara. This means that he was at a disadvantage, since it was his first time in the Kitchen Stadium, while Hagiwara had already experienced a battle there. He was also the only Iron Chef that had to include a pasta dish in his menus: he was a "prince" with many handicaps and obstacles.

In his own field, however, he was an unbeatable prince. After his disaster with Hagiwara, he was victorious over all Italian challengers. He also won most of the battles against Chinese and multicultural chefs.

The fact that he never lost two battles in a row must be commended. The only other Iron Chef who never lost consecutively are Ishinabe and Michiba. Had he been able to keep this up for the Special Battles, his deviation value would certainly have improved. Unfortunately, the only Special Battle he took part in was the Strongest Iron Chef Battle.

The Third Japanese Iron Chef: Masaharu Morimoto

Overall Results

Type of Battle	Win/Lose/Tie	Winning Rate (percent)
Overall (24 battles)	16/7/1	67
Tag Match	0/0/0	
Versus a Revenger	1/0/0	100
Versus an Iron Chef	0/2/0	0
Special Battles (1 battle)	0/1/0	0

- **Longest winning streak: 4 battles**

- **Total points: 52**

- **BG deviation value: 2.17**

Results for Different Theme Ingredients

Ingredient	Win/Lose/Tie	Points	BG Deviation Value
Seafood	8/3/1	25	2.08
Vegetable	3/3/0	12	2.00
Meat	1/0/0	0	3.00
Other	4/1/0	12	2.40

Results against the Challengers

Cuisine	Win/Lose/Tie	Points	BG Deviation Value
French	3/1/0	9	2.25
Japanese	9/5/1	31	2.07
Italian	0/1/0	0	0.00
Chinese	1/0/0	3	3.00
Multicultural	3/0/0	9	3.00

When the new Iron Chef of Japanese Cuisine, fresh from New York, marked his debut, it was a very impressive sight. Because of his image, Morimoto's low deviation value of 2.17 is a bit of a letdown. This is probably due to the fact that, like Kobe, he did not appear on the Special Battles too often. This score is understandable, given that Morimoto competed in only 24 battles, through no fault of his own.

He lost his first Special Battle against Sakai in the Strongest Iron Chef Battle. The victory over a Revenger was against Hiro Yamashita, who he had tied before. Overall, Morimoto's score is not bad. He has topped Chen and Nakamura in certain genres of challengers and theme ingredients. He won all three battles against the multicultural chefs. The only blemish is his loss against the Italian chef Marco Molinari. Had he won this battle, he would have won a majority of his battles in all themes and genres. It would have also meant that his winning streak would have been seven battles. If only the theme ingredient had not been porcini . . .

Gourmet Academy's
Glossary of Culinary Terms

Aigyoku jelly: An egg custard.

Amadai: Tilefish.

Amiabura: Diaphragm of pork and mutton; a net-like membrane used to cover ingredients.

Angler: Monkfish.

Ankimo: Monkfish.

Anzu: Apricot.

Arai: A type of sashimi. Cold running water cools thin slices of raw fish, so that the meat becomes constricted.

Asatsuki: Green onion.

Ayu: Sweetfish.

Balsamic vinegar: Vinegar from the Modena region in Italy; the main ingredient is stewed grapes. Its color is black; it smells like wine.

Béchamel sauce: White sauce of flour sauteed with butter and thinned with milk.

Bei nasu: Deep-fried.

Black pork: A breed of pig that has very flavorful and tender meat.

Blanch: To boil vegetables and organ meat quickly.

Bouillabaisse: A dish from Provence, France; a fish soup flavored with oil, tomatoes, and saffron.

Bouillon: Meat or vegetable stock; available dried.

Caramel: Reduced liquid sugar. The sugar is reduced over a heat of 150° to 170°.

Carpaccio: Originally, sauce over thin raw slices of meat. Thin slices of fish are used these days as well.

Carre d'agneau: The underside of a lamb's rib.

Caviar: Salted fish roe (eggs). Sturgeon roe is considered the best. One of the three delicacies of the world.

Cercle: A round shape (French).

Champignon: Mushrooms (French).

Chao: To saute.

Cheng: To cook ingredients with indirect steam; the ingredients are placed in a steaming basket.

Chevreuil: Venison.

Chili sauce: Tomato-based sauce with salt, vinegar, and chili powder.

Chyon tsai: Sauteing ingredients over very high heat with oil.

Cocotte: Round or oblong pot with a cover; also refers to a dish.

Collaie: The entrails of sea scallops or the miso of prawns and crabs.

Compote: Fruits cooked in syrup.

Concasser: To mince roughly with knives.

Consommé: The soup resulting after cooking vegetables and meat in a bouillon.

Crème brulée: Pudding with a caramelized surface.

Crepin: See *amiabura*.

Daikon: Giant white radish.

Dashi: All-purpose soup stock.

Demi-glace: Sauce made with a base of brown sauce (sauteed bacon and vegetables cooked with roux and tomato puree) and reduced stock.

Dim sum: Chinese snack.

Dragee: Almonds with a hard sugar coating.

Escalope: Thin slices of meat or fish.

Eva milk: Pasteurized unsweetened condensed milk; packed in cans.

Fettuccini: Flat pasta.

Flambé: A technique in which liquor (brandy) is poured into a pan and then set on fire; the flavor and smell of the liquor are left in the dish.

Foie gras: French for fat (gras) liver (foie). The liver of well-fattened ducks and geese. Foie in French means liver, and gras means fat. One of the three world delicacies.

Fond de veau: Veal stock.

Fruit de mer: Ingredients from the sea (French); shellfish and crustaceans.

Garniture: Accompaniment; garnish.

Gâteau: Baked desserts and cakes with floured crust.

Girolle: Chanterelle mushroom.

Glacé: To brown or saute vegetables in sugar, butter, and water.

Glacé au truffes: Truffle ice cream (French).

Gusokuni: To cook shellfish with their shells intact.

Gyoza dumpling: Potsticker; wonton sheets filled with ground meat or vegetables.

Hamo: An eel-like fish found almost exclusively in Western Japan.

Harabiraki: Filleting a fish into one piece by cutting it from the belly.

Hina matsuri: Girls' Festival celebrated on March 3rd. On this day, families with girl children invite friends and relatives over, serve special food and drink, and wish for the girls to grow healthy and beautiful.

Hiragai: Also called penshell clam, fan shell clam, razor shell clam, and sea clam; they are common in Japan.

Hirami: Flounder.

Homard: Lobster.

Huopao: Technique used in Chinese cooking; set the contents of the pot on fire to get rid of excess water and oil.

Ikomi: A technique in which the insides of a vegetable are spooned out, or cut open, so that ingredients can fill the interior.

Ikura: Salmon roe.

Jus de truffe: Truffle juice.

Kaiseki: Japanese sampling menu of delicacies.

Kakushibocho: To cut the underside of an ingredient to allow the heat and flavors to go through better.

Kame: Turtle.

Kanpyo: A dried gourd.

Karasumi: Dried mullet roe; one of the three delicacies of Japan.

Katsuo dashi: Bonito stock.

Keiji: Baby salmon.

Keshyojio: A technique used to grill fish; placing salt on the tail and fins of a fish before grilling to prevent them from burning.

Kinome: Young leaves of the prickly ash; often used as a garnish.

Kobujime: To lightly salt a fillet of fish, lay it on kelp, and cover it with more kelp so that the seaweed flavor is transferred to the fish; used mainly for white fish without a strong smell, like sea bream and sea bass.

Kome nasu: rice with eggplant.

Konbu: Kelp or sea tangle; a dark brown seaweed. Also called kombu.

Konnyaku: Devil's tongue jelly; a starchy, gelatinous cake made of a tuber.

Kouglof: A dessert from the Alsace region that is shaped into a crown; anything shaped like a crown.

Kuchiko: Dried sea cucumber roe; one of Japan's three delicacies.

Mariné: Marinate (French).

Mascarpone: Unheated type of cream cheese from the Lombardi region of Italy; used in desserts like tiramisu.

Matsutake: Pine mushroom.

Mentori: Blunting the edges of cut vegetables to help the vegetables retain their shape while being cooked.

Meringue: Sweetened whipped egg whites.

Merunière: Fish coated with flour and sauteed in butter.

Millefeuille: A type of cake, with custard in between layers of pie crust.

Milt: Soft roe; see *shinjo*.

Minegiri: To pound on an ingredient using the back of the knife.

Mirin: Sweet cooking wine made from rice.

Mise en place: Prepeparation; also whole preparation of a meal.

Miso: Fermented bean paste.

Mochi: Glutinous rice cake.

Moiji oroshi: ground/grated.

Mousse: Foam (French); a dish made of whipped egg whites and whipped cream; may be sweet or savory.

Mozzarella: Cheese made of water buffalo's or cow's milk.

Namako: Button-like mushroom.

Namplar: Fish sauce from Thailand.

Nanbanzuke: Fried fish and meat with a chili vinaigrette sauce.

Nappé: To spread a creamy ingredient on something.

Natto: Steamed, fermented mashed soybeans.

Nikogori: Cold and solidified cooking stock.

Nyokunam: Fish sauce from Vietnam.

Osechi: Traditional Japanese New Year's dish. Although there are a lot of varieties of osechi, it is traditionally packed in a four-tiered lacquer box called a "jubako."

Pao: A term meaning to cover.

Parmesan: A hard cheese; the king of Italian cheeses.

Pâté: Minced meat, fish, or vegetables baked in skin or in a bowl.

Pidan egg: Also called a 1000-year-old egg.

Poire: To cook using butter or oil in a frying pan.

Ponzu soy sauce: Dressing for vinegared foods; a dipping sauce.

Puree: Ingredients liquefied in a blender.

Roast: To cook in an oven.

Ronkonkai chicken: A special chicken raised in Jiangsu, China.

Roux: Flour sauteed with an equal amount of butter; used as a base for many sauces.

Sabaillon: Cream sauce made of egg yolks, sugar, and wine.

Saignante: To cook a meat rare.

Sake: Rice wine.

Sasagaki: A technique used mainly for long vegetables such as carrot and burdock. To scrape the vegetable while rotating it, like sharpening a pencil.

Sashimi: Sliced raw fish.

Sauce perigord: A sauce made of Madeira wine and truffles.

Saury: A type of pike.

Sebiraki: To cut open a fish from its back.

Shabu-shabu: A dish similar to beef fondue; meats and vegetables cook in boiling broth.

Shallots: Small oblong type of onion; its flavor is a cross between onion and garlic.

Shark's fin: The dried back, breast, and tail fins of a shark.

Shinjo: Steamed or grilled ball of minced fish. Egg white, yam, salt, and dashi are added to the fish.

Shirako: Soft roe; the testicles of a fish.

Smoke: A method of drying and steaming fish and meat.

Soba: Buckwheat.

Softshell crab: A crab caught just after shedding its old shell, when its new shell is still forming.

Sorbeture: An ice cream freezer used to make ice cream and sherbets.

Sujime: A technique for preparing fish; sprinkling salt lightly on both sides of a fillet, letting it stand for a while, then washing the salt out. After the fillet dries, it is seeped in vinegar until the surface turns white.

Sushi: Raw fish with vinegared rice.

Takiawase: A dish with more than two types of boiled items. Each ingredient is cooked in a different type of stock to best enhance its flavor.

Tamari soy sauce: A dark, thick soy sauce.

Tan tsai: A soup dish.

Tartar sauce: Sauce made of mayonnaise, shallots, herbs, hard-boiled eggs, onions, and pickles.

Tartar steak: Minced raw beef with herbs.

Terrine: A dish cooked in a terrine-shaped dish.

Touchih: Chinese condiment made with fermented soy beans; used in sautees and steamed dishes.

Toupanchiang: Miso made of chili, fermented horse beans, and spices.

Tournage: A technique of cutting vegetables.

Truffle: A very fragrant mushroom; one of the three delicacies of the world.

Tsai: Dish (Chinese).

Udon: Wide/thick Wheat noodles.

Ume: Plum.

Umeboshi: Pickled plum.

Uni: Sea urchin; one of the three delicacies of Japan.

Vapeur: To steam.

Wakame: Lobe-leafed seaweed.

Warishita: A flavoring made of dashi, sake, mirin, sugar, and soy sauce; used for soup in hotpot dishes.

Wasabi: Horseradish.

Wine vinegar: Vinegar made from grapes; available in red and white forms.

XO chiang: A Chinese sauce made of dried shell ligaments, dried shrimp, Chinese ham, and chili mixed with oil.

Yamato patato: Japanese mountain potato.

Yuba: Dried soy milk skin.

Yugama: Yuzu used as a platter; the top two thirds of a yuzu are cut off and the insides are scooped out.

Yusen: Double boiler.

Yuzu: Citron; a sour citrus fruit used primarily for its rind.

RESTAURANT GUIDE

THERE IS ONLY ONE BETTER way to experience *Iron Chef* than to watch the show, and that is to actually eat the food prepared by these men and women of culinary skill. For that reason, we've included this brief restaurant guide.

We begin with the Iron Chefs, then follow with the challengers from the United States and Canada. Also, in order that they might gain the people's acclaim forever, we have included as many of the victorious challengers as we could. Unfortunately, thanks to the difficulty of this task, we could not include all of the winners. And obviously, because of the nature of the restaurant business, some of the information will have changed since this list was compiled.

We have, however, done our best.

Iron Chefs

Yutaka Ishinabe

Born in 1948, in Yokohama City, Kanagawa-ken. Entered the culinary world at the age of 16 and apprenticed all over Japan. Returned to Tokyo at 18 years old and joined "Frére Jacques" as a chef. Increased business at this restaurant, and spread his name as an intelligent, able chef. Shortly afterward, left for France and studied there, furthering his abilities as a chef. Returned to Japan 5 years later, at the age of 27. Opened his own restaurant, Queen Alice, in 1984, at the age of 34.

The Queen Alice Guesthouse, near the Queen Alice, is designed according to Ishinabe's taste. He personally helped in the interior design and chose all the dishware. The result is a restaurant with a charming ambience. There is a wide variety of dishes to choose from, and the flexibility is pleasing. Not confining himself to cooking just French, Ishinabe has now ventured into Chinese and ethnic cuisines.

Name of restaurant: Queen Alice Guesthouse

Phone: 03-5411-0900

Address: 3-2-33 Nishi Azabu, Minato-ku, Tokyo

Hours: 12:00 P.M.–1:30 P.M.; 6:00 P.M.–8:30 P.M.

Open: throughout the year

Credit Card: accepted

Reservations: needed

Prices: 3,500 yen (lunch)/7,500 yen (dinner).

The Visconti of the

French culinary

world

Rokusaburo Michiba

Born in 1931, in Ishikawa prefecture, to a family that dealt in tea cere-
mony objects. Interested in cooking since childhood; especially particular about the type of dishware used to serve his dishes. Apprenticed in
famous restaurants in Kobe, Kanazawa, and Tokyo. After working at
Akasaka's Akasaka Jobanya, opened, at age 40, the Ginza Rokusan-Tei in
Ginza, where culinary connoisseurs flock.

The ambience of the Ginza Rokusan-Tei is calming. There are several tables, as well as counter seats. It is on the eighth and ninth floors of
a building in Ginza. There is a clear view of the kitchen from the seats on
the eighth floor. Here you will have the opportunity to view Michiba,
known as "the god of Japanese cuisine" and "the rebel of the culinary
world," in action. He also owns the Poisson Rokusaburo, which is more
relaxed, with an open kitchen.

Name of restaurant: Ginza Rokusan-Tei

Phone: 03-3571-1763

Address: Dai San Sowaredo Building, 8th & 9th floors, 8-8-7 Ginza,
Chyuo-ku, Tokyo

Hours: 5:00 P.M.–9:00 P.M.

Open: Monday–Saturday; closed holidays

Credit Card: accepted

Prices: 12,000 yen (Rokusan course, dinner)/15,000 yen (dinner).

A free-thinking

philosopher of cuisine,

not bound to the

regiments of genre

Chen Kenichi

Born in 1956, in Tokyo. His father, Chen Kenmin, introduced Szechwan cooking to Japan and created the much-loved "shrimp in chili sauce." Popular Chinese dishes today, like the hoho chicken and mabo tofu, are based on Szechwan cooking. Inherited his father's Japanese-style Szechwan cooking.

After graduating from Tamagawa University, apprenticed in Shisen Hanten (Szechwan Fandian).

At the Akasaka Shinsen Hanten, Szechwan cooking, called the world's most progressed cooking, and Chen's philosophy of "Cooking is love" can be experienced. Real Szechwan cooking, being too spicy for most other palates, has been refined. Chen is responsible for running the Shisen Hanten group, now found in Akasaka, Ikebukuro, Kisarazu, Hiroshima, and Ogura.

Name of restaurant: Akasaka Shisen Hanten

Phone: 03-3263-9371

Address: Zenkoku Ryokan Kaikan, 5th & 6th floors, 2-5-5 Hiragacho, Chiyoda-ku, Tokyo

Hours: 11:30 A.M.–2:00 P.M.; 5:00 P.M.–9:00 P.M.

Open: throughout the year; closed at year end and New Year's

Credit card: accepted

Other: private rooms available

Prices: 7,000 yen (lunch, dinner)/5,000 yen (buffet, party of 30 +)/à la carte available.

"Cooking is love." He

offers happiness

through food.

IRON CHEF

Hiroyuki Sakai

Born in 1942 in Kagoshima Prefecture. Interested in cooking since child-hood. Always determined to be a financially successful chef. Joined the Shin Osaka Hotel in Osaka as an apprentice at the age of 17. At 19, flew to Australia to apprentice at the Hotel Oriental for a year and a half. Upon returning to Japan, apprenticed for 3 years at the restaurant Shiki in the Ginza district, under the late Fujio Shiwata. After working as a chef at Aoyama's Coco Palms and Roppongi's John Kanaya, opened his own restaurant La Rochelle in Aoyama at the age of 38. The shop later moved to Shibuya.

The view from the restaurant, situated on the 32nd floor, is spec-tacular. While guarding the tradition of French cuisine, Sakai is flexible enough to try new types of dishes. The result is a hearty, romantic cook-ing, unlike anything anywhere else. Sakai has plans to open a restaurant in New York City in the near future.

Name of restaurant: La Rochelle

Phone: 03-3400-8220

Address: Toho Seimei Building, 32nd floor, 2-15-1 Shibuya, Shibuya-ku, Tokyo

Hours: 12:00 P.M.–2:30 P.M.; 6:00 P.M.–9:00 P.M.

Open: Tuesday–Sunday

Credit card: accepted

Prices: 2,800 yen (weekday lunch)/3,300 yen (weekend & holiday lunch)/8,500 yen (dinner)

The Delacroix of the

French culinary

world

Koumei Nakamura

Born in 1947 in Shimabara City, Nagasaki Prefecture. Entered the culinary world at the age of 18; apprenticed in restaurants such as the Oriental Hotel in Osaka. At 33 years of age, joined the restaurant Nadaman in the Hotel New Otani. After working as the head chef of Nadaman Singapore in the Shangri La Hotel, returned to Japan at the age of 45. Became the manager of Nadaman in the Hotel New Otani.

Nakamura's original style of cooking, reflecting his time in Singapore, is an eclectic mix of Chinese and French qualities. He has succeeded in creating his own world of Japanese cooking. He has now opened his own restaurant, Koumei, in Ariake. This new restaurant, with its tranquil interior, is a place where one can experience both the traditional and avant-garde flavors of Japanese food.

Name of restaurant: Koumei Ariake

Phone: 03-3599-3636

Address: Ariake Park Building, 2nd floor, 3-1-28 Ariake, Koto-ku, Tokyo

Hours: 11:00 A.M.–3:00 P.M.; 5:00 P.M.–9:00 P.M.

Open: throughout the year

Credit card: accepted

Prices: 1,200 yen (lunch)/3,500 yen (dinner)

The second Iron Chef

Japanese: a chef

whose skill has been

recognized by

Michiba

IRON

Katsuhiko Kobe

Entered the world of Italian cuisine upon his graduation from university. In 1994, joined the Italian restaurant known as the epitome of Italian cooking, the Enoteca Pinccioli in Florence.

At his new restaurant customers will be able to taste Kobe's classic, yet creative cooking.

Name of restaurant:	Ristorante "Massa"
Phone:	03-5452-0502
Address:	1-23-11 Ebisu, Shibuya-ku, Tokyo
Hours:	11:30 A.M.–1:30 P.M.; 6:00 P.M.–9:30 P.M.
Open:	Thursday–Tuesday
Credit card:	accepted
Prices:	2,000–4,000 yen (lunch)/6,000–10,000 yen (dinner)

Having honed his
skills in an elite
restaurant in Italy,
he is the Prince of
the Italian culinary
world.

Masaharu Morimoto

Entered the world of sushi as an apprentice at the age of 18. In 1984, moved to New York where he first joined the Sony Club as the head chef of Japanese food. Went on to become the head chef at Robert De Niro's famous restaurant, Nobu.

The Father of Neo-Japanese cuisine will be opening his own restaurants in Philadelphia and New York City. Morimoto (723 Chestnut Street, Philadelphia) will be opening in Spring 2001 and the New York restaurant is scheduled to open later in the year.

The Basquiat of the culinary world, he creates a progressive world of Japanese cooking relying on his flexible concepts.

IRON CHEF

American and Canadian Challengers

Patrick Clark

A pioneer of New American cooking, who combined classic French technique with traditional down-home Southern cooking, and added a distinctive New York City flair.

Patrick Clark discovered his love of cooking early. As a young boy growing up in Brooklyn, he spent much time in the kitchen with his mother, and often visited the hotel kitchens where his father worked as a chef. He began his professional education at New York City Technical College, then traveled abroad to train at Great Britain's Bournemouth Technical College. After working at several restaurants in Europe, Clark returned to the States to develop his unique style of contemporary American cuisine. He served as executive chef at several restaurants including New York City's Odeon; Bice in Beverly Hills; the Hay-Adams Hotel in Washington, D.C.; and his own Metro. He was even asked to become executive chef at The White House, but he turned down that position. Instead, Clark took the helm at New York's famous Tavern on the Green, where he stayed until November 1997. In February 1998, Patrick Clark died of cardiac arrest at the age of 42. His culinary career was cut short, but his legacy lives on.

Bobby Flay

Top New York chef and star of The Food Network, Bobby Flay was chosen to defend the honor and prestige of American cuisine in the New York Battle. Iron Chef Morimoto emerged victorious, but Chef Flay has earned the American people's ovation and fame forever.

Bobby Flay fell into cooking at the age of 17, when he took a job at Joe Allen's restaurant in New York City where his father was a partner. Mr. Allen was so impressed with Flay's natural ability that he paid his tuition to The French Culinary Institute. Flay later received the first "Outstanding Graduate Award" in 1993, and now acts as spokesperson and Master Chef for the school. His first job as executive chef, at New York City's Miracle Grill, caught the attention of restaurateur Jerome Kretchmer who offered Flay the opportunity to open the critically laud-

ed Mesa Grill in 1991. Flay then teamed with partner Laurence Kretchmer in November 1993 to open Bolo. Bolo was awarded two stars by the *New York Times* in 1994 and continues to be voted the top Spanish restaurant in New York City by the Zagat Survey. But Chef Flay's acclaim extends far beyond New York. He is the author of three bestselling cookbooks and is a favorite on The Food Network, where he launched and starred in three national cooking shows: *Hot Off the Grill with Bobby Flay, Grillin' and Chillin'*, and his most recent, *Food Nation*.

Name of restaurant: Mesa Grill

Phone: (212) 807-7400

Address: 102 Fifth Avenue, New York, NY 10011

Hours: Lunch: Monday–Friday; 11:30 A.M.–2:30 P.M.

Dinner: Sunday–Thursday; 5:30 P.M.–10:30 P.M.; Friday & Saturday; 5:30 P.M.–11:00 P.M.

Brunch: Saturday & Sunday; 11:30 A.M.–3:00 P.M.

Credit cards: All major credit cards accepted

Lunch: $35

Dinner: $55

Restaurant: Bolo

Phone: (212) 228-2200

Address: 23 East 22nd Street, New York, NY 10010

Hours: Lunch: Monday–Friday 11:30 A.M.–2:30 P.M.

Dinner: Sunday–Thursday 5:30 P.M.–10:30 P.M.; Friday & Saturday 5:30 P.M.–11:00 P.M.

Closed for lunch on Saturday & Sunday

Credit cards: All major credit cards accepted

Lunch: $35

Dinner: $55

Noda Minoru

The Japanese American walked proudly into Kitchen Stadium carrying the American flag, ready to fight for his country.

Minoru, head chef of a Los Angeles restaurant called Hanabishi, faced Iron Chef Michiba in Battle Matsutake Mushroom. The Iron Chef was victorious, but Minoru made a valiant effort. Despite numerous attempts, the editors of this book were unable to gather any information about Chef Minuro or Hanabishi. We think the restaurant is still open, but it is very difficult to get in touch with them.

Name of restaurant: Hanabishi

Phone: (213) 687-3193

Address: 114 S. Central Avenue, Los Angeles, CA 90012

Wayne Nish

A chef whose extensive training and culinary talent have combined with his innately creative vision to make him one of America's most innovative chefs.

He began his culinary career at the Quilted Giraffe and La Colombe d'Or in New York City. In August 1990, he opened March, in a turn of the century town house in midtown Manhattan with coowner/host/wine director Joseph Scalice. They recently completed a $2 million renovation and expansion at March, transforming it into a tri-level luxury establishment with a rooftop terrace for outdoor drinking and dining. Nish's prix fixe tasting menus—available with or without paired wines from Scalice's award-winning wine list—reflect his unique and innovative New-American culinary style with global influences. He is currently at work on a March cookbook.

Restaurant: March

Phone: (212) 754-6272

Address: 405 East 58th Street (between 1st Avenue & Sutton Place), New York, NY

Hours: Dinner only 6:00 P.M.–11:00 P.M. seven days a week

Credit card: All major credit cards

Prix Fixe Tasting Menus (from 4 course w/o wine to 7 course with wine): $72–$196

Michael Noble

A Canadian culinary ambassador in Japan and at home

The only Canadian to challenge the Iron Chefs, Michael Noble is the executive chef at the Metropolitan Hotel and its award-winning restaurant, Diva at the Met. Within its first year, Chef Noble propelled Diva into Vancouver's culinary spotlight, earning recognition with a slate of awards, and the Canadian Federation of Chefs & Cooks named Chef Noble 1999/2000 Chef of the Year. He is impassioned by the use of fresh and organic local ingredients as much as he is inspired by global finds. He practices a philosophy that ingredients should be balanced and uncomplicated to keep flavors honest.

Restaurant:	Diva at the Met and the Metropolitan Hotel
Phone:	(604) 687-1122
Address:	645 Howe Street, Vancouver, BC V6C 2Y9
Hours:	Breakfast: Monday–Friday 6:30 A.M.–11:00 A.M.
	Brunch: Saturday & Sunday 7:00 A.M.–11:00 A.M.
	Lunch: Monday–Friday 11:30 A.M.–2:30 P.M.
	Dinner: Every evening 5:30 P.M.–10:00 P.M.
Credit card:	All major credit cards are accepted
Lunch:	(average cost for an entrée) CA $19.00
Dinner:	(average cost for an entrée) CA $33.00

Michael Noble's Iron Chef Tuna

Tougarashi seared tuna with potato and gobo root soup

SERVES 4

FOR THE SOUP

$^1\!/_2$ onion, sliced

$^1\!/_2$ cup gobo root, peeled and sliced

1 stalk of celery, sliced

4 white mushrooms, sliced

$^1\!/_2$ leek, sliced

1 clove garlic, minced

3 tbsp. butter

1 tsp. flour

1 potato, cubed

1 liter hot chicken stock

salt and pepper to taste

50ml cream

juice of $^1\!/_2$ lime

METHOD

In a soup pot over moderate heat, melt the butter then saute onions until translucent. Add the gobo root, celery, mushroom, leek, and garlic and continue sauteing until soft. Sprinkle the flour over the vegetables and stir to combine. Add the chicken stock and bring to a simmer. Cook the soup for approximately 15 minutes and then add the potato. Bring back to a simmer and continue cooking another 10 minutes. Place the hot soup in a blender and carefully blend until pureed. Past the blended soup through a fine strainer. Bring the soup back to a simmer; season to taste with salt and pepper. Add cream and lemon juice and remove from heat.

FOR TUNA

200 gr. sashimi grade tuna, cut into 1½" × 5" pieces

20 ml grape seed oil

salt and pepper to taste

dash of Tougarashi spice*

*Tougarashi spice is found in Asian markets

METHOD

Coat the tuna with grape seed oil. Season with salt, pepper, and Tougarashi. Sear the tuna in a very hot pan until all sides are charred and tuna is still "rare" inside. Set aside.

FOR THE SALAD

3 red skin potatoes, cooked in salted water or steamed, then chilled

15 ml grape seed oil

6 baby corn (raw), sliced on a bias

8 cherry tomatoes sliced in half then dried in a slow oven

frisee greens

mizuna salad or other mustard greens

4 slices of thinly sliced cucumber, formed into a collar

sherry vinegar, to taste

salt and white pepper, to taste

METHOD

Cut the potatoes into small wedges. In a skillet over moderate heat, sauté the potatoes in the grape seed oil until they are lightly browned. Set aside to cool to room temperature. In a mixing bowl, place the potatoes, corn, tomatoes, frisee, and mizuna. Dress with sherry vinegar to taste.

TO ASSEMBLE THE DISH

Take four soup bowls and place three slices of tuna on the bottom of each. Place cucumber collar on top of tuna and fill with salad. Carefully ladle the hot soup into the bowl, around the tuna, until it comes to the top of the tuna slices without covering.

Serve immediately and enjoy.

Ron Siegel

The first and only American chef to beat the Iron Chef, Siegel has become a celebrated icon in Japan.

Ron Siegel entered the food business at the tender age of 16 when he took a job in the butcher department of a small San Francisco grocery. At the age of 20, his skillful butchering abilities helped him land his first position as prep cook in a neighborhood restaurant. He slowly began to develop an affinity for food, eventually working his way up to the rank of cook in several restaurants in the area. Spending time in different kitchens made Siegel realize how much he enjoyed cooking. He decided to formalize his education by attending classes at the California Culinary Academy. After spending time at restaurants in California and New York City, Siegel accepted the position of Executive Chef at Charles Nob Hill in San Francisco. There he has created a menu of contemporary French cuisine with local California influences and indulges his diners with imaginative creations made from such luxury foods as oysters, caviar, lobster, foie gras, quail, duck, crab, squab, and abalone, mixed with the freshest seasonal ingredients. Siegel's talent for putting a creative spin on time-honored French classics has made him one of the country's greatest chefs and triumphant in Kitchen Stadium.

Restaurant: Charles Nob Hill

Phone: (425) 771-5400

Address: 1250 Jones Street, San Francisco, CA 94109

Hours: Tuesday–Thursday 5:30 P.M.–10:00 P.M.
Friday & Saturday 5:30 P.M.–10:30 P.M.
Sunday 5:30 P.M.–9:30 P.M.
Closed Mondays

Credit cards: Visa, MasterCard, Diners Club, American Express

Price range: $9–$23 for appetizers, $26–$34 for entrees, $8–$12 for desserts. Six-course tasting menu $70; 9-course tasting menu $100; the sommelier's wine pairing $45 per person

"If ever a challenger wins over the Iron Chef, he or she will win the people's ovation and fame forever."

Ron Siegel took on Iron Chef Hiroyuki Sakai for Battle Lobster in 1998. His five-course meal was a culinary masterpiece and he left Kitchen Stadium triumphant and with the honorary title of Iron Chef.

The meal that claimed victory in Battle Lobster:

- **Lobster Custard with Beluga Caviar**

- **Lobster Soup with Black Truffles and Sauteed Scallops**

- **Grilled Lobster Salad with Avocado, Tomato Conasse, and Basil Oil**

- **Lobster Ravioli with Corn Juice, Sweetbread Medallions, and Sauteed Abalone**

- **Oven Roasted Lobster with Seared Foie Gras, Braised Artichokes, Wild Mushrooms, Port, and Fig Jus**

Lobster Custard with Beluga Caviar

1 cup milk

1 cup cream

3 whole eggs

¹/₂ cup lobster stock

1 oz. Beluga caviar

2 pounds rock salt

1 pound mixed spices (fresh bay leaves and peppercorns)

METHOD

Bring milk and cream to a boil with lobster stock. Remove eggs from shell by cutting off the tops. Once removed from the shell, temper the liquid with the eggs. Season with salt and pepper. Strain through chinois. Cut the tops off 7 more eggs, and empty out the egg from the shell. Clean eggshell, removing the membrane with your finger. Rinse in warm water. Place empty shells back in egg carton on a large casserole pan. Fill pan with water until it is just touching the bottom of the eggs (about ¼ of egg should be in the water). Fill shells with custard. You are baking in a water bath. Cover and bake at 275° for 40 minutes.

TO PLATE

Place custards on a bed of rock salt and spices. Add your caviar on top and serve.

Lobster Soup with Black Truffles and Sauteed Scallops

1 quart lobster stock

4 scallops, still in their shells

1 oz. black truffles

1 pint cream

Salt and pepper

METHOD

Make a flavorful lobster stock using 20 lobster shells, 20 fresh tomatoes, and tarragon with water to cover. Reduce stock down to 1 quart and strain through chinois. Remove scallops from shell and season with salt and pepper. Sear scallops in pan. Chop black truffles fine. Dice the seared scallops. Add cream to lobster stock and simmer for 10 minutes. Season stock with salt and pepper.

TO PLATE

Add chopped scallops and black truffles to your soup cups. Pour hot soup over and serve.

Grilled Lobster Salad with Avocado, Tomato Concassé, and Basil Oil

3 whole lobsters

2 avocados

2 lemons

Olive oil

Salt and pepper

4 whole tomatoes

5 bunches of basil

1 oz. chervil

½ bunch parsley

20 chive points

½ bunch tarragon

METHOD

Split lobster tails in half, season with salt and pepper, lightly brush with olive oil. Place on grill. Blanch tomatoes in boiling water for ten seconds. Place in bowl of ice to cool. Peel skins off tomatoes and dice. Place in strainer to drain all liquid from tomatoes. Peel avocado and slice in half. Cut halves into half-moons. Take basil and blanch in boiling salt water for ten seconds, refresh in ice water. Ring out excess water, then place in a bar blender with 1 cup olive oil. Puree for 5 minutes. Once pureed, place in a strainer to catch the pulp. You want to save the oil. Remove lobster meat from the shells. Season and brush lightly with oil and grill. Once grilled, toss the claws and tails with lemon to taste and olive oil. Pick all the fresh herbs from stems and place in a bowl. Toss the diced tomatoes with salt, pepper, and olive oil.

TO PLATE

Layer on plate in the following order: diced tomatoes, avocado, lobster, and fresh herbs. Drizzle basil oil on top.

Lobster Ravioli with Corn Juice, Sweetbread Medallions, and Sauteed Abalone

3 whole lobsters

1/2 cup mascarpone cheese

Salt and pepper

8 ears of corn

6 sweetbread medallions

1 live abalone

1 oz. chervil

1/4 bunch tarragon

1/4 bunch basil

1 bunch chives

1/4 bunch parsley

1/4 bunch thyme

2 sheets pasta

1 egg

METHOD

Dice up lobster meat. Chop herbs, toss with mascarpone and lobster. Season with salt and pepper. Set mixture aside in the refrigerator until needed. Juice 8 ears of corn, and strain. Take abalone out of shell, clean and slice thin, then julienne and sauté with fresh chives. Sauté sweetbread medallions, dusting them first with flour. Make your ravioli with lobster filling. Use an egg to eggwash the sheets together. Cut out ravioli with desired cutter. Blanch ravioli in boiling water. Slowly cook corn juice until it is reduced to a sauce consistency. Season with salt and pepper.

TO PLATE

Layer in the following order in a bowl: corn sauce, ravioli, sweetbread medallion, and sauteed abalone

Oven Roasted Lobster with Seared Foie Gras, Braised Artichokes, Wild Mushrooms, Port, and Fig Jus

6 lobster tails

4 artichokes

6 2 oz. pieces of foie gras

3 cups assorted wild mushrooms

1 bottle port

6 large figs

1 bunch chives

1 bunch thyme

3 garlic cloves

4 pounds butter

METHOD

Clean artichokes so that all you have left are the hearts. Cut each piece into sixths. Cook in lemon water. Dice up mushrooms and saute with 2 tablespoons butter, thyme, salt, and pepper. Put port in a pan and reduce by ⅔, then add fresh figs to port for about ten minutes, then remove. Add fresh black pepper to reduction, enough so that you taste the pepper, then add 1 tablespoon butter. Melt 4 pounds butter with 1 bunch thyme and 2 cloves garlic. Season the lobster tails with salt and pepper, then add to melted butter and cook for 5 minutes. Sear off foie gras.

TO PLATE

Place artichokes and mushrooms down in middle of plate, then add poached figs on top. Put lobster down next, then the foie gras. Drizzle the plate with port sauce and serve.

Victorious Challengers from Asia and Europe

Masamitsu Takahashi (Challenger 49)

Apprenticed in a top level Kyoto restaurant for 8 years, since the age of 18. After apprenticing in restaurants in Hakata and Kochi, opened his own restaurant, Takahashi, in Akasaka when he was 40.

Only natural, fresh ingredients shipped straight from the local areas are used in Takahashi's restaurant. If such ingredients cannot be had, he will turn down even Yeltsin's reservation. His dishes are steeped in the traditional Kyoto style of cooking.

Name of restaurant:	Takahashi
Phone:	03-3244-9806
Address:	2-17-52 Akasaka, Minato-ku, Tokyo
Hours:	11:30 A.M.–1:30 P.M.; 5:30 P.M.–10:30 P.M.
Open:	Monday–Saturday; closed holidays
Credit card:	not accepted
Prices:	1,200–7,000 yen (lunch)/5,000–35,000 yen (dinner)

A missionary of Kyoto cuisine, he has succeeded in impressing Yeltsin.

Tetuo Hagiwara (Challenger 228)

Younger son of Uotoku, a restaurant owner in Kagurazaka. Wanted to be a professional bowler until the age of 22. At 25, opened his restaurant, Menosou.

Hagiwara carries on the Edo tradition of "chic" in his cooking, yet his cooking isn't presumptuous. Instead of relying on his skills, he concentrates on bringing the best out of every ingredient.

Name of restaurant:	Menosou
Phone:	03-3267-8180
Address:	4-3 Kagurazaka, Shinjuku-ku, Tokyo
Hours:	5:30 P.M.–10:00 P.M.
Open:	Monday–Saturday; closed holidays
Credit card:	not accepted
Reservations:	required for lunch
Prices:	5,000 yen (lunch)/10,000 yen (dinner)

A true Edo chef, he never forgets the importance of chic in his cooking. He never lets himself rely solely on his skills; rather, he concentrates on bringing the best out of every ingredient.

Takatugu Sasaoka (Challenger 256)

Started with the restaurant Hasegawa; apprenticed at many of Japan's top restaurants. At 35, opened his restaurant Sasaoka in Tangenji.

Sasaoka follows the teachings of Rosanjin. Most important are his words "Cooking is not about destroying the ingredient's flavors." He even uses wine at times to create spectacular dishes.

Name of restaurant: Sasaoka

Phone: 03-3444-1233

Address: Nakamura Building 1F, 2-17-18 Ebisu, Shibuya-ku, Tokyo

Hours: 12:00 P.M.–1:00 P.M.; 6:00 P.M.–9:00 P.M.

Open: Monday–Saturday; closed holidays and the second and fourth Saturday of the month

Credit card: all but Amex accepted

Prices: 3,000–5,000 yen (lunch)/8,000–10,000 yen (dinner)

An ardent follower of Rosanjin's teachings, he is the Prince of Japanese cuisine.

Tooru Komori (Challenger 274)

Honed his skills by working at different restaurants in Nihonbashi and Shinbashi since the age of 18. Member of the 178-year-old Housei-kai; student of Edo cuisine. At 48, became the head chef of Keyaki-tei.

Komori's cooking is based on his skilled use of the knife. Delicate tastes, as well as the heart of Edo, can be experienced through his dishes.

Name of restaurant: Japanese Restaurant Keyaki

Phone: 03-5467-1421

Address: Jubilee Plaza Building 4F, 5-8-5 Jingumae, Shibuya-ku, Tokyo

Hours: 11:30 A.M.–2:00 P.M.; 5:00 P.M.–10:00 P.M.

Open: Monday–Saturday

Credit card: accepted

Prices: 2,500–7,000 yen (lunch)/8,000–15,000 (dinner)

He is the man, armed with his extensive knowledge of the usage of knives, who will help Edo cuisine progress.

Tomitoku Syuu (Challenger 8 & II)

Apprenticed, since the age of 18, at Chugoku Hanten. At 28, became the subhead chef of Keio Plaza Hotel's Nanyuan. At 37, made the head chef of Heichinrou, located in Yokohama.

Shu takes seasonal ingredients and elevates their taste to such a level that it never fails to impress even the most critical. He challenged Michiba in order to avenge his brother's loss.

Name of restaurant: Canton Meisai Tomitoku

Phone: 03-3497-3111

Address: CI Plaza B1F, 2-3-1 Kita Aoyama, Tokyo

Hours: 11:00 A.M.–9:30 P.M.

Open: throughout the year

Credit card: accepted

Prices: 1,000–1,500 yen (lunch)/15,000+ yen (dinner)

A genius of Chinese cooking, he controls the "world of food heaven."

Yuuji Wakiya (Challenger 33 & 174)

At 15 years old, joined Sanno Hanten in Akasaka. Became the assistant to the head Chinese chef of Hilton Hotel at 25 years old. At 27, became the head chef of Tachikawa's Recent Park Hotel. At 37, joined forces with the Honorary Iron Chef Ishinabe to create Turandot, a restaurant that serves French-Chinese cooking. Became head chef of this restaurant.

Wakiya is also adept at creating French and Italian dishes. His dishes, summed up in a word, are elegant.

Name of restaurant: Turandot

Phone: 045-682-0361

Address: Pan Pacific Hotel Yokohama, 2-3-7 Minatomirai, Nishi-ku, Yokohama, Kanagawa

Hours: 11:30 A.M.–2:30 P.M.; 5:30 P.M.–9:00 P.M.

Open: throughout the year

Credit card: accepted

Prices: 3,500 yen (lunch)/7,500 yen (dinner)/à la carte menu available

A genius of nouvelle Chinois, he is the young rebel of Chinese cuisine.

Meisei Sou (Challenger 84)

Started his apprenticeship at Shinbashi's Shisenhanten at the age of 18. At 22, joined Huandu Fandian in Mita. The next year, promoted to head chef. At around that time, started going to the Imperial Household as the Chinese chef.

Sou cooks dishes that were served in the Chinese Court and that are based on Szechwan cooking. He also incorporates Cantonese elements in his cooking, creating original dishes that do not bore your palette. His skills can now be experienced at his restaurant Mihi.

Name of restaurant: Mihi

Phone: 03-3453-3676

Address: 4-12-39 Shibaura, Minato-ku, Tokyo

Hours: 11:30 A.M.–2:00 P.M.; 5:00 P.M.–9:00 P.M.

Open: Monday–Saturday; closed holidays

Credit card: accepted

Prices: 900–1,500 yen (lunch)/3,000–20,000 yen (dinner)

The envoy of the mother of Chinese cooking, Mrs. Ma, he is also the chef for the Imperial Family.

Zyukyou Ryou (Challenger 231 & 232)

Commenced apprenticeship at 20 years old, 2 years after his older brother, Zyunou. At 40, furthered his studies under his brother's tutelage at the Okura Hotel. Went on to become the head chef of Tori in the Hotel Nikko Osaka. Became the head chef of Tougu at the Hotel Nikko Tokyo at the age of 54.

Ryou's cooking is a synthesis between the old and the modern and reflects the true image of Cantonese cooking, which has always been one step ahead of the times.

Name of restaurant: Tougu

Phone: 03-5500-5500

Address: Hotel Nikko Tokyo 2F, 1-9-1 Daiba, Minato-ku, Tokyo

Hours: 11:30 A.M.–2:30 P.M.; 5:30 P.M.–9:30 P.M.

Open: throughout the year

Credit card: accepted

Prices: 2,500+ yen (lunch)/7,000+ yen (dinner)

The younger brother of the renowned Ryou brothers of Cantonese cuisine.

Kaken Sya (Challenger 262)

Apprenticed in over 40 restaurants in Hong Kong since the age of 13. Made the head chef of Heichinrou in Hibiya at the age of 32. At 46, promoted to director/executive head chef of Heichinrou.

Sya's dishes are indisputably art itself, owing to his extensive knowledge and mastery of the skills. He has elevated further the tradition with his gracious and dynamic cooking.

Name of restaurant:	Heichinrou
Phone:	045-681-3001
Address:	149 Yamashitacho, Naka-ku, Yokohama, Kanagawa
Hours:	11:30 A.M.–11:00 P.M.
Open:	throughout the year
Credit card:	accepted
Price:	1,200–2,500 yen (lunch)/5,000+ yen (dinner)

The master of Heichinrou, his dishes are a true reflection of the traditions of a renowned establishment.

Gyokubun Sai (Challenger 273)

Started her apprenticeship at Peking Szechwan Hanten, a restaurant catering to the Chinese government. Soon became famous for her skills, and quickly found herself cooking for Mao Tse Tung, Chou En Lai, and other VIPs from all over the world.

The secret of Sai's cooking lies in the usage of an ingredient's natural flavors to the fullest. It is a fine example of Pekinese court cooking.

Name of restaurant: Kanmeiho

Phone: 03-3224-1607

Address: Akasaka New Plaza 105, 7-6-47 Akasaka, Minato-ku, Tokyo

Hours: 11:00 A.M.–2:30 P.M.; 5:30 P.M.–10:00 P.M.

Open: throughout the year

Credit card: accepted

Prices: 1,000–3,800 yen (lunch)/5,000+ yen (dinner)

Holder of the Culinary Expert license, regarded in China as the ultimate license. She is revered as a god in her home country and is a national treasure level chef.

Takeshi Ookubo (Challenger 278)

Started his apprenticeship at the age of 18 and exhibited his skillfulness at celebrated Cantonese restaurants. Met Kihachi Kumagai when he was 36 years old. Became the head chef of Kihachi China in Ginza at the age of 38.

Ookubo's strength lies in his imaginative use of multicultural elements. More than 200 different sauces from all over the world are utilized.

Name of restaurant:	Kihachi China Ginza
Phone:	03-5524-0761
Address:	2-3-6 Ginza, Chuo-ku, Tokyo
Hours:	11:30 A.M.–2:30 P.M. (lunch); 11:30 A.M.–4:00 P.M. (Sunday); 5:30 P.M.–9:30 P.M. (dinner)
Open:	throughout the year
Credit card:	accepted
Prices:	2,700+ yen (lunch)/5,500+ yen (dinner)

Recognized as a master of Cantonese cuisine by the restaurant Kihachi, he employs sauces from all over the world in his dishes.

Jacques Borie (Challenger 10)

Apprenticed at Le Grand Vefour since 1960; came to Japan in 1973. Continued his apprenticeship at the Hotel Okura. In 1983, awarded the MOF. Became the head chef of L'Osier in 1986.

Borie rejected the kaiseki-style French cuisine and has remained loyal to the classic dishes of French cuisine.

Name of restaurant: L'Osier

Phone: 03-3571-6050

Address: 7-5-5 Ginza, Chuo-ku, Tokyo

Hours: 12:00 P.M. (lunch); 5:30 P.M. (dinner)

Open: Monday–Saturday; closed holidays

Credit card: accepted

Prices: 4,800–7,500 yen (lunch)/14,000–25,000 yen (dinner)

He won the French award for best chef, the MOF.

Kyouko Kagata (Challenger 21 & 25I)

After graduating from the Woman's Nutritional College in 1990, accepted an offer from the Royal Park Hotel. Under Mitsuo Shimamura's tutelage, went on to win the Toque D'or contest as the youngest ever to do so.

Kagata's dishes go beyond what the recipe calls for and shine in their artistry. Feminine touches are evident in her presentation.

Name of restaurant: Restaurant Goji

Phone: 03-5428-1250

Address: 15-8 Hachiyamacho, Shibuya-ku, Tokyo

Hours: 11:30 A.M.–2:00 P.M.; 5:30 P.M.–10:00 P.M.

Open: throughout the year

Credit card: accepted

Prices: 1,200–2,000 yen (lunch)/900–3,200 yen (dinner)

The first female chef to appear on the show, she was also the youngest chef to be victorious.

Tadaaki Shimizu (Challenger 37)

Joined La Tour D'argent after going to France at the age of 24. After returning to Japan at the age of 27, appointed to vice head chef of the Japanese branch of La Tour D'argent; became the vice head chef of the French branch at age 28. Two years later, made head chef of the Japanese branch. Opened la Tourelle when he was 38 years old.

Shimizu's dishes are classical, with many uses of artistic sauces. Perfect dishes are available for a very reasonable price.

Name of restaurant:	La Tourelle
Phone:	03-3267-2120
Address:	6-8 Kagurazaka, Shinjuku-ku, Tokyo
Hours:	11:30 A.M.–2:30 P.M.; 6:00 P.M.–10:00 P.M.
Open:	Tuesday–Sunday
Credit card:	accepted (dinner only)
Prices:	2,500+ yen (lunch)/7,000–10,000 yen (dinner)

He was the first Japanese to become the vice head chef of the world's most famous French restaurant.

Joel Bruant (Challenger 38)

Born in France. Started studying French cuisine at the age of 13. Joined the restaurant Paul Bocuse at 19 years old. Appointed as vice head chef at the age of 24. The same year, came to Japan as executive head chef of Rengaya. Opened his restaurant, Joel, at 32 years old. Your five senses will be thrown into throes of ecstasy after experiencing Bruant's skillful dishes and delightful sauces, which are strongly influenced by Bocuse.

Name of restaurant: Joel

Phone: 03-3400-7149

Address: Kyodo Building, 2nd floor, 5-6-24 Minami Aoyama, Minato-ku, Tokyo

Hours: 12:00 P.M.–2:30 P.M.; 6:00 P.M.–10:00 P.M.

Open: throughout the year

Credit card: accepted

Other: Sea Bass Pie available à la carte (13,000 yen for two servings) if reserved in advanced

Prices: 3,800–7,000 yen (lunch)/8,000–18,000 yen (dinner)

The beloved student of the Emperor Paul Bocuse, his sauces and skills delight your five senses.

Artur Rütter (Challenger 45)

Mastered the basics of French cooking at Germany's National Culinary School. Apprenticed in exotic places, such as onboard a luxury liner. After serving as the executive head chef of a restaurant in Cannes, embarked on a round-the-world culinary apprenticeship. Appointed as the personal chef to the mayor of Paris at the age of 25. Came to Japan at the age of 48 and opened Chez Sylvia.

Rütter's dishes, derived from designs he creates, are small pieces of art.

Name of restaurant: Chez Sylvia

Phone: 0424-74-3426

Address: 15-6-101 Higashi Honcho, Higashi Kurume-shi, Tokyo

Hours: 11:30 A.M.–2:00 P.M.; 5:00 P.M.–10:00 P.M.

Open: Wednesday–Monday; closed first and third Mondays of the month

Credit card: not accepted

Prices: 5,000 yen (lunch)/10,000 yen (dinner)

The genius from Germany, who has mastered cuisines from around the world.

Etuo Jou (Challenger 81 & 173)

Made the head chef of Lecrin in Ginza at 32 years old. Became well-known around this time. Opened Vincent at 45 years old.

It is said that there were never any leftovers on the plates of dishes that he created. Jou's authentic French dishes, which weigh heavily on sauces, remain fiercely loyal to tradition.

Name of restaurant: Vincent

Phone: 03-3589-0035

Address: Inac Bldg. B1F Building, B1 floor, 5-18-23 Roppongi, Minato-ku, Tokyo

Hours: 11:30 A.M.–2:00 P.M.; 6:00 P.M.–10:00 P.M.

Open: throughout the year; closed first and second Sundays of the month

Credit card: accepted

Prices: 3,500–6,000 yen (lunch)/7,500–12,500 yen (dinner)

A big weight of the Club de Trente, he is known as the Jou of Sauces.

Kazutaka Okabe (Challenger 83)

Began his study of French cuisine at the age of 19. Goes to France when at 25. Before his deportation due to an expired visa, travels around the country, learning the skills of French cooking. Becomes the executive head chef of Enoteca in Hiroo after his return to Japan.

Not overly concerned by the beauty of a dish, Okabe expresses the myriad charms of each ingredient in a dynamic manner.

Name of restaurant: Okabetei

Phone: 03-3479-5452

Address: Grand Maison Nogizaka B1F, 1-15-19 Minami Aoyama, Minato-ku, Tokyo

Hours: 11:30 A.M.–2:30 P.M.; 6:00 P.M.–10:00 P.M.

Open: Monday–Saturday

Credit card: accepted

Prices: 2,500–4,000 yen (lunch)/4,800–7,800 yen (dinner)

He goes to the Tsukiji Fish Market by bicycle from Hiroo. He expresses the charm of each ingredient in a dynamic manner.

Toyoaki Suganuma (Challenger 128)

Finds his way to France at the age of 24; rejected by all the restaurants there. Undeterred, becomes a sushi chef at a sushi restaurant. The following year, succeeds in joining Le Duc. At 26, becomes the head chef of the Pierre Cardin Guest House. Opens his restaurant in Shimokitazawa, Le Grand Comptoire, at age 34 and is the executive head chef. Suganuma's ability allows him to create a classical, yet avant-garde cuisine.

Name of restaurant: Le Grand Comptoir

Phone: 03-3410-7645

Address: Suehiro Building, 2nd floor, 2-15-15 Kitazawa, Setagaya-ku, Tokyo

Hours: 11:30 A.M.–2:00 P.M.; 5:00 P.M.–9:00 P.M.

Open: throughout the year

Credit card: accepted

Prices: 2,000–5,000 yen (lunch)/5,000–10,000 yen (dinner)

A chef of astounding ability, he seeks to bring out the chamber music of French dishes.

Philippe Batton (Challenger 137)

Apprenticed in Paris since the age of 15. During that time, met the master chef Philippe Grout. Came to Japan when he was 27 as a chef at the Royal Park Hotel Palazzo. Becomes the executive head chef of Evelyne at the age of 32.

Batton's classic yet innovative dishes outshine those of the other chefs.

Name of restaurant: Le Petit Bedon

Phone: 03-5457-0086

Address: Hillside West A B1, 13–13 Hachiyamacho, Shibuya-ku, Tokyo

Hours: 11:30 A.M.; 6:00 P.M.

Open: throughout the year

Credit card: accepted

Prices: 3,600+ yen (lunch) / 5,000–6,000 yen (dinner)

One of the top French Chefs in Japan despite his young age.

Toshiyuki Nakajima (Challenger 199)

Joined La Maree when he was 20 years old. At 24, joined Akasaka's Hikari-tei. At 25, he went to France and the United States and spent 2 years apprenticing abroad. Returning to Japan, worked at Amapora, La Pure Piece in Nishi Azabu, and finally settled at Restaurant Lo a la Bush, becoming head chef.

Using seasonal ingredients, Nakajima's dishes are kind to the body.

Name of restaurant: The House of 1999 Restaurant L'eau a la Bouche

Phone: 03-3498-3001

Address: 4-2-9 Shibuya, Shibuya-ku, Tokyo

Hours: 11:30 A.M.–1:30 P.M.; 6:00 P.M.–9:00 P.M.

Open: throughout the year

Credit card: accepted

Prices: 3,500–6,500 yen (lunch)/7,000–15,000 yen (dinner)

He is a chef that sends out delicate dishes in touch with the changing seasons.

Keiji Azuma (Challenger 208)

Went to France at the age of 26 and apprenticed at Trois Gros and other famous restaurants. Returned to Japan at 30 years of age; became the head chef of L'ile de France.

Azuma's dishes, heavy on sauces, convey the yesteryears of France. His charm lies in the authentic, classical dishes.

Name of restaurant: L'ile de France

Phone: 03-5485-2931

Address: Taihan Building, 2nd floor, 3-6-23 Kita Aoyama, Minato-ku, Tokyo

Hours: 11:30 A.M.–2:00 P.M.; 6:00 P.M.–9:30 P.M.

Open: throughout the year

Credit card: accepted

Prices: 1,500–3,500 yen (lunch)/2,500–9,000 yen (dinner)

Earning the acclaim of the French, his dishes are authentic and are not swayed with the times.

Hiromi Yamada (Challenger 27)

Began his apprenticeship at the age of 18; went to Italy when he was 28 years old. Returned to Japan and accepted a position as head chef of Pasta Pasta. Opened his own restaurant in Nishi Azabu named Vinocchio at the age of 35. After a car accident, left the culinary world for a period of time. Three years later, appeared on *Iron Chef* and revealed a legendary dish, which was forever etched in our memory.

Yamada now pursues his own style of Italian at Ristorante Hiro.

Name of restaurant: Ristorante Hiro

Phone: 03-3486-5561

Address: T Place B1F, 5-5-25 Minami Aoyama, Minato-ku, Tokyo

Hours: 12:00 P.M.–1:30 P.M.; 6:00 P.M.–8:30 P.M.

Open: throughout the year; closed for lunch on Mondays and Tuesdays

Credit card: accepted

Prices: 1,800–4,800 yen (lunch)/ 6,500–8,000 yen (dinner)

The legendary chef

who created

"cold pasta."

Kouji Kobayashi (Challenger 52)

At 22 years of age, commenced his study of Italian cuisine. Joined the renowned Vissani in Italy when he was 30. At 30, promoted to the position of head chef. Became a truck driver when he returned to Japan in 1991.

Never creating the same dish twice, Kobayashi's cooking is based solely on the inspiration he feels when he lays his eye on an ingredient.

Name of restaurant: Marie	
Phone: 03-3446-9700	
Address: New Towa Building, 1st floor, 5-2-9 Minami Azabu, Minato-ku, Tokyo	
Hours: 12:00 P.M.–2:00 P.M. 6:00 P.M.–11:00 P.M.	
Open: Monday–Saturday; closed holidays	
Credit card: accepted	
Prices: 1,800–4,800 yen (lunch)/6,000–7,500 yen (dinner)	

He is a legendary chef, as well as the beloved pupil of Italy's genius Gianfranco Vissani.

Takamasa Uetake (Challenger 148)

Started working at Belle Mare at the age of 20. Later worked at Pasta Pasta in Harajuku. Made his way to Italy at the age of 25. Became the personal chef at the summer house of Benetton's owner. Returned to Japan at the age of 30; became the executive head chef of Bigollosso.

Uetake's dishes, made of numerous types of olive oil, are worth the experience.

Name of restaurant: Canoviano

Phone: 03-5456-5681

Address: 2-21-4 Ebisu Nishi, Shibuya-ku, Tokyo

Hours: 12:00 P.M.–2:00 P.M.; 6:00 P.M.–10:00 P.M.

Open: Tuesday–Sunday

Credit card: accepted

Prices: 3,000 to 5,000 yen (lunch)/6,500 to 8,000 yen (dinner)

A true magician manipulating over 100 different olive oils harvested from the symbol of peace, the olive tree.

Hironobu Tujiguchi (Challenger 267)

Started his apprenticeship at the age of 18. Went to France at the age of 30 to further his skills. Won prestigious awards both in Japan and overseas. In 1997 won the world cup of desserts, the Coupe de Monde.

Tujiguchi leads the path to a new era of pastries with his liberated ideas.

Name of restaurant: Mont Saint Clair

Phone: 03-3718-5200

Address: 2-22-4 Jiyugaoka, Meguro-ku, Tokyo

Hours: 11:00 A.M.–6:00 P.M. (coffee shop); 11:00 A.M.–7:00 P.M. (cake shop)

Open: Thursday–Tuesday; closed the third Tuesday of the month

Credit card: not accepted

Prices: 650 yen (tea)/200–500 yen (cake)

A young genius who has stood at the peak of over 10,000 patissiers.

Tadamichi Ota (Challenger 110)

Joined Nakanobo Zuien, located in Arima Onzen, as its head chef in 1981. In 1982, appointed Vice Chairman of the Japanese Culinary Association, an association with over 20,000 members.

There is no chef in Japan who does not know of Ota's name. His cooking style is not conservative; rather his novel ideas and sensitivity create an avant-garde style.

Name of restaurant: Nakanobo Zuien

Phone: 078-904-0781

Address: 808 Arimamachi, Kita-ku, Kobe-shi, Hyogo-ken

Hours: 11:30 A.M.–3:30 P.M. (day trip); 1:00 P.M.–12:00 P.M. (overnight trip)

Credit card: accepted

Prices: 18,000+ yen (day)/30,000+ yen (overnight)

With 300 disciples, he reigns over the Ota faction from the inner chamber of Kansai.

Miturou Harada (Challenger 226)

Began his apprenticeship at the age of 18. Developed his skill in various renowned restaurants. Appointed head chef of Yoshida Sanso at 38 years old. In 1985, became the head chef of Kyoto Brighton Hotel Hotaru.

Harada breathes new life into the heart of Kyoto cuisine with his new and novel dishes.

Name of restaurant: Hotaru

Phone: 075-441-4411

Address: Nakadachiuri, Shinmachi, Kamigyouku, Kyoto-shi, Kyoto

Hours: 7:00 A.M.–10:00 A.M.; 11:00 A.M.–12:30 P.M.; 5:00 P.M.–10:00 P.M.

Credit card: accepted

Prices: 2,000–3,700 yen (lunch)/8,000+ yen (dinner)

He carries on his back the reputation of a first-class hotel.

Yoshimi Tanigawa (Challenger 286)

Started his apprenticeship in Kyoto at the age of 15. Working at various restaurants, mastered the art of Kyoto cuisine. At 31, opened his own restaurant in the Shimokamo area of Kyoto.

Tanigawa guards the basic belief of Kyoto cuisine by preparing dishes so that the flavors of the ingredients are straightforward. There are no extra frills on his dishes; they are purely to be enjoyed for their taste.

Name of restaurant: Kichisen

Phone: 075-711-6121

Address: 5 bancho, Tadasunomori, Shimogamo, Sakyoku, Kyoto-shi, Kyoto

Hours: 12:00 P.M.–3:00 P.M.; 4:30 P.M.–10:00 P.M.

Open: throughout the year

Credit card: not accepted

Prices: 8,000 yen (lunch)/14,000 yen (dinner)

He prepares the most sophisticated Kyoto cuisine in all of Kyoto.

Kazuhiko Tei (Challenger 6)

Graduated Nan High School and Kansai Gakuin University. Mastered culinary arts in Taiwan and Hong Kong. At 24 years old, became the chef of Ryoutan. Has served as lecturer of Japanese television's *Today's Cooking* for 35 years.

With pride in his vast knowledge and experiences, Tei claims "there must be two sides to cooking; attacking and protecting." He was victorious over Kenichi during Battle Octopus, with his skillful mastery over the live animal.

Name of restaurant: Mr. Tei's Taiwanese Restaurant Ryutan

Phone: 06-6341-3040

Address: Osaka Ekimae Dai 3 Building B1F 1-1 Umeda, Kita-ku, Osaka

Hours: 11:30 A.M.–10:00 P.M.

Open: Monday–Saturday

Credit card: accepted

Prices: 630–1,260 yen (lunch)/4,000 yen (dinner)

A chef at the peak of the Kansai Chinese world, he was the first to ever win against an Iron Chef.

Kazunari Takada (Challenger 210 & 211)

Entered, at the age of 29, Kanazawa's Tsuruko as a chef in charge of boiled dishes. There mastered the art of Kaga cuisine. Opened his restaurant Toshihisa at 36 years old.

Takada creates flawless dishes that satisfy the discerning palettes of the people of Kanazawa. His dishes, derived from dashi, are straightforward but bottomless in their depth.

Name of restaurant:	Toshihisa
Phone:	0762-47-4111
Address:	4-13-37 Arimatsu, Kanazawa-shi, Ishikawa-ken
Hours:	11:30 A.M.–2:00 P.M.; 5:00 P.M.–9:00 P.M.
Open:	Thursday–Tuesday
Credit card:	accepted
Prices:	2,500–5,000+ yen (lunch)/8,000–15,000 yen (dinner)

He carries with him the future of the tradition of Kaga cuisine.

Fumiaki Satou (Challenger 219)

Started his apprenticeship at the age of 18; became the executive head chef of Motoyu at Ureno Onsen in Saga in 1991.

Sato's creations and the vessels create a harmonious unit. His skills, worthy of the beautiful receptacles, uphold the basics of Japanese cooking. Exceptional dishes created with the abundant harvests of Saga can be experienced here.

Name of restaurant: Ureshino Onsen Motoyu Hatsuhana

Phone: 0954-42-1200

Address: 2202-8 Ooaza Shitayadocho, Ureshinomachi, Fujitsu-gun, Saga-ken

Hours: 11:30 A.M.–1:30 P.M.; 5:00 P.M.–8:30 P.M.

Credit card: accepted

Prices: 2,000–5,000 yen (lunch)/3,000–10,000 yen (dinner)

A "manipulator of receptacles," he appreciates the essence of Arita-yaki.

Takeshi Kajimoto (Challenger 240)

Started his apprenticeship at the age of 18; learned the basic skills of dashi. Served as a chef of boiled dishes. In 1993, became the head chef of Tokiwa in Yamaguchi Yuda Onsen.

One of the characteristics of Kajimoto's dishes is his constant pursuit of new and innovative flavors. At the base of this pursuit is his utilization of dashi made from various types of konbu.

Name of restaurant:	Nishi no Miyabi Tokiwa
Phone:	0839-22-0091
Address:	4-6-4 Yuda Onsen, Yamaguchi-shi, Yamaguchi-ken
Hours:	11:00 A.M.–3:00 P.M. (day trip); 3:00 P.M.–10:00 P.M. (overnight trip)
Credit card:	accepted
Prices:	6,000+ yen (day)/ 15,000–35,000 yen (overnight)

A virtuoso of konbu seaweed, he is constantly in pursuit of new and innovative flavors.

IRON CHEF

Seiya Masahara (Challenger 272)

Commenced apprenticeship at the age of 18; taught the basics of Japanese cuisine by master chef Tadamichi Oota at Arima Onsen's Nakanobo Zuien. At 33, became the head chef of Yuhara Grand Hotel Hakkei in Okayama.

Masahara's dishes are traditional, using a wealth of mountain harvests. This characteristic is evident in his seasonal hotpots.

Name of restaurant: Yuhara Grand Hotel Hakkei

Phone: 0867-62-2211

Address: 1572 Houei, Yuharamachi, Maniwa-gun, Okayama-ken

Hours: 11:30 A.M.–2:30 P.M. (day trip); 3:00 P.M.–10:00 P.M. (overnight trip)

Credit card: accepted

Reservations: required for weekdays

Other: ask about weekend hours

Prices: 5,000+ yen (day) 17,000–23,000 yen (overnight)

A master of dishes cooked in pots, he excels in the foundation of Japanese cooking.

Takaya Nakazawa (Challenger 120)

Joined Honkon-en in Meguro at 22 years old. At 44, journeyed to China and perfected his mastery of his original sauces. Striving to outdo the late Chen Kenmin, created over 50 different sauces, all of which are artistic.

Nakazawa's habitual words are, "be nice to your ingredients, be nice to your customers." He is a pioneer of a new Chinese cuisine frontier.

Name of restaurant: Chinese Restaurant Sanchou, Rikuchyabo

Phone: 0559-78-1021

Address: 614 Hirai, Kannamicho, Tagatagun, Shizuoka-ken

Hours: 11:30 A.M.–2:00 P.M.; 5:00 P.M.–8:00 P.M.

Open: February, April, June–December

Credit card: not accepted

Prices: 2,700+ yen (lunch)/4,000–9,000 yen (dinner)

Unable to forget his experience of Chen Kenmin's chili prawns, he continues to pursue the re-creation of Kenmin's flavors.

Hiroshi Yamanobe (Challenger 116)

Went to France at the age of 23, committing to his memory the flavors of France. Returned to Japan and apprenticed at restaurants such as Lecant in Ginza. Became executive head chef of Hayama's La Maree de Chaya, the restaurant responsible for the Shonan boom. Yamanobe is presently the head chef of Chez Yamanobe located in Fukushima. French cuisine, centered around the freshest ingredients, can be sampled here.

Name of restaurant: Chez Yamanobe

Phone: 0241-68-3585

Address: 1316 Tatemoto otsu, Yunokami Aza, Ooaza, Shimosatocho, Aizu-gun, Fukushima-ken

Hours: 12:00 P.M.; 6:00 P.M.

Open: throughout the year; may be closed on holidays

Credit card: accepted

Prices: 3,500–5,000 yen (lunch)/8,500–10,000 yen (dinner)

He single-handedly guarded the culture of Shonan back in the 1980s.

Acknowledgments

Special thanks to:

Yukio Hattori
Atsushi Nakayama
Akihiko Saito
Tsukihiko Sato
Fumihiko Sakai
Tomoyuki Sekiguchi
Kiyoyuki Ichimaida
Setsuko Yuuki
Tatsuo Ito
Keiko Enseki

Manami Mizutani
Isshin Ogaeri
Hideaki Takahashi
Michiko Nakamura
Keiko Kawashima
Tomoyuki Yoshida
Yuusuke Oodate
Dai Mitsuya
Hattori Nutrition College
All the challengers and their
restaurants

IRON CHEF